D0367400

DANCING...
For A Living

Where The Jobs Are
What They Pay
What Choreographers Look For
What To Ask

By
Don Mirault

Rafter Publishing   *Toluca Lake, California*

DANCING... For A Living

By Don Mirault

All rights reserved. No part of this book may be reproduced or transmitted in any form or by any means, electronic or mechanical, including photocopying, recording or by any information storage and retrieval system without written permission from the author, except for the inclusion of brief quotations in a review.

Copyright © 1993 By Don Mirault
Printed in the United States of America

Library of Congress Catalog No. 93-85551
ISBN 0-9637864-4-X
$15.95 Softcover

Rafter Publishing
11333 Moorpark Street
Suite 141
Toluca Lake, California 91602

ACKNOWLEDGMENTS

First and foremost, I want to thank Sheri, for realizing I was doing something when it looked like I was doing nothing. To Sy Fischer, who inspired me with the words "You're a fool if you don't". Thanks to Juliet Doran, without her this book would still be in my head. To my editor–in–chief, Keith Sellon–Wright, whose editorial notes were sometimes longer than the book. Special thanks to Gwen Feldman and K Callan, who were very helpful to a total stranger. Most of all, thanks to the many choreographers, Entertainment Directors and agents who gave their time and knowledge because, like me, they love The Dancer.

Cover by: Ron Duran

Table of Contents

Chapter Six - LAS VEGAS PRODUCTIONS   113

Chapter Seven - MTV / MUSIC VIDEO   141

CHAPTER ONE

THE HORROR STORY

We absolutely nailed the audition, even the lifts. My partner and I were called before the choreographer. In a moment we had the payoff to hours of practice and pain. We had — a job!

The answers to questions came rapidly. A three month run at $400.00 a week, round trip airfare, no passport – just a birth certificate. You will be working on the top floor of Fiesta Palace, a beautiful hotel resort. The nightclub has a 270–degree view of Mexico City from twenty–four stories above. You leave in three days. WOW!

We arrived in Mexico with our American group of eight consisting of a choreographer, six tall blonde beauties and myself. I was feeling really good at this point. We were taken through customs, asked more than once if we were Swedish athletes and introduced to our Producer. He seemed a warm, friendly man. He looked at the women, grabbed his heart and spoke in broken English, "Angels, I must be in Heaven!"

The Producer drove us to a government building where we had to fill out forms for work visas.

"They're valid for six months and you must have one to work in Mexico," said the clerk.

We were given copies of our visas by the Producer and instructed to keep them with us at all times.

We adapted quickly to our new life. Rehearsals flew by, the show opened and was a hit. The choreographer, satisfied with a job well done, flew back to the United States and I finally had the time to enjoy Mexico.

The sites, the food, the customs and the people were wonderful. I made every effort to meet the people and learn their ways, and looking like a 'Swedish athlete' made it that much more fun.

The show was performed to sold out crowds and we were extended for an additional three months. We were given the option of continuing on in Mexico or heading home to the U.S. We were having a great time, not to mention putting some money away... the entire cast stayed on.

I started to branch out in Mexico, dancing in some television specials and I even managed a couple of weekend trips to Acapulco, (a twenty–five minute flight). Now I was living!

On the fifth month of our stay we were notified that the show would be extended for yet another three months. This time I was torn. Although I was happy, I was lonely for the sight of a Burger King or a Shell gas station. My partner and I decided to give a four week notice, stating we would leave at the end of our six month contract.

Two weeks passed and our replacements arrived from Las Vegas. They were two young dancers who had met for the first time on the plane. I was in shock! We had only two weeks to teach partner work that had taken us almost a year to perfect.

With no additional pay we rehearsed our replacements six hours a day and performed at night. We taught, re–choreographed and guided Sheryl and John through their new dance numbers every day of our last two weeks.

Opening night arrived and we were scheduled to fly to Vegas the following morning. This time rather than performing, my partner and I sat in the audience with the Producer, feeling like expectant parents.

The show began. It was rough, but I thought the dancers did one helluva job. As the curtain fell the Producer leaned over to me and said, "They were unacceptable, we're not letting you go."

I laughed, taking his remark as a 'joking compliment' and headed backstage to give corrections and encouragement.

The day of our departure arrived. We said our good–byes to the other dancers, grabbed our bags, and headed for the International section of the airport. It's funny, I was as excited about going home as I was about arriving.

I handed the agent our airplane tickets, the copies of our work visas and birth certificates.

"These work visas are no good," the agent said. "I must have the original."

"What!" I informed him where we were working and that all we were given were copies.

"Well, you can understand that there could be twenty copies of this work visa, and I couldn't allow all twenty people to leave the country."

My anger started to boil as my thoughts turned to the Producer who knew we couldn't get out of the country and yet let us pack and go to the airport. I also recalled what he'd said to me the night before, 'We're not letting you go'... It wasn't a joke. The seriousness of the situation struck me.

In an act of desperation, I asked the agent, "How much would it take to get us on that plane?" stating it as if I'd done this a hundred times before.

"I couldn't possibly accept anything," he replied.

The words just hung in the air. Bribes in Mexico had always been so readily accepted, or so I had thought.

Feeling deflated, depressed and very angry, we returned to the hotel where I immediately got on the phone with the Producer and introduced him to some of the vocabulary I learned in the Navy. It didn't faze him. He started to negotiate with me! How much more money would I like? A larger hotel room? Maybe an apartment?

It had nothing to do with money, housing or Mexico. We felt it was time to return to the States and hopefully find other work, and I told him so. He hung up on me! That did it! I was no longer a rational person. He now had a tiger in a cage.

The show was dark that evening, so the entire cast was in my room trying to figure out the available options. They ranged from going to the U.S. Embassy to burning down the showroom. We chose the former.

The next morning at 10:00 AM sharp, we approached the U.S. Embassy. It was rather intimidating. Ringing the bell, I felt like a little kid eating a peanut butter and jelly sandwich on the back porch of the White House.

We were ushered in and briefly explained our situation to the first person who'd listen. We were told to wait. A few minutes later a door opened and we were introduced to an assistant to the Ambassador. He invited us in to an office that looked just like I'd seen in the movie "MISSING".

Nervously, I explained our situation. He listened carefully and then proceeded to say what I'd also heard in the movies.

"All I can do is fill out forms to be mailed to the Mexican government requesting that they let you out of the country."

"Requesting!" My voice rose two octaves higher than normal.

"I'm sorry. It's their country. It's all I can do."

I thanked him and left feeling Spanish was no longer going to be my second language.

That night as the show was on I sat in my hotel room wondering how all this had happened and promised myself that it would never happen again. Tossing and turning in my bed, I got an idea, a weird one, but a glimpse of hope nonetheless.

We could fly from Mexico City to Tijuana, take a cab to the border and walk across to the States using our driver's licenses as ID's. Sure, it was drastic, but these had become drastic times.

The phone rang. It was the Producer's Assistant. In a cool tone of voice he let us know how ungrateful we were. He went on to say that the Producer would rather not have 'trouble makers' in his hotel. I held my pride in check.

"Your work visas will be at the front desk in the morning." They were. The ordeal was over.

EXPERIENCE IS NOT ALWAYS THE BEST TEACHER

I flew home relieved but angry. Angry with the Producer, but surprisingly, angry with myself. How could I have let this happen? Of course, I had never worked out of the country before, never had a work visa, so it never crossed my mind that only the original was valid. I had trusted the Producer for information I should have known. Don't misunderstand, the Producer was not doing anything illegal by holding the original work visas. I've found that many Producers try to hold work visas or passports of their dancers in foreign countries because unhappy dancers have been known to fly home in the middle of a run. The producers are left with their show closing and the loss of capital. They are trying to protect their investment.

I feel we should try to protect our investment... ourselves.

With Mexico behind me and lessons learned, I was trying to think of a way to save other dancers the pain I went through. I wondered if there was a way to teach new dancers various bits of information. Info learned from the experiences of other dancers that could save them hours of stress and heartache. Experience is a good teacher but often a painful one. I also thought it ironic that new groups of dancers were leaving for foreign countries with the same lack of knowledge, falling prey to the same mistakes I did, days, months, or years before.

The only way useful information is passed on to the dancer is by word of mouth. But for the new dancer, or the dancer heading to New York or Los Angeles for the first time, word of mouth is unacceptable.

These were the reasons for writing this book.

YOU ARE THE AGENT

Dancers love to dance. They live it, love it, and talk about it constantly. The joy of dance is difficult to express in words, but I feel that this joy and love for 'The Art' can sometimes compromise the knowledge of the business in which we work. There should be room in the heart of every dancer to learn some of the 'business' in the 'Show Business' we love so much.

One of the realities to dancing is that, unless you work on the Equity Stage, excel in commercials, or happen to dance in union films, (all covered later) chances are, you will not have an agent. A dancer performing union work without an agent is still protected by the strict guidelines and minimums of the union, but a dancer performing non–union work without an agent is subjected to many more variables and unknowns. This is the reason non–union work is stressed in this edition.

The purpose of this book is to inform you of the things you should know about in the types of work you are going to be involved in. "Where is the work?" "What types do they look for?" "What are the benefits?" "What do I need to know?" All these questions will be answered.

Although few dancers are in a position to negotiate money, there are many things you can negotiate and get!

How Do I Know When I'm Ready?

Ah, the age old question. It is a real possibility that every dancer has asked it at one time or another. It reminds me of a question we all asked as young people... "How will I know when I'm in love?" It's funny how the person answering that question always stumbles for a moment and then says, "Oh, you'll just know."

That same answer holds true for the dancer, you'll just know. This is not a flippant or uncaring solution to a practical question. The fact that you feel in your heart that it's time to move to Los Angeles or New York to make a living as a dancer, may be a good indication that you truly are ready. But, is it enough? Even though most dancers are hopeless romantics (or you wouldn't be in this business), we need to explore some other reasons for moving into the 'Big Time'. Reasons that are practical and logical.

PREPARING FOR YOUR MOVE

If you are an experienced dancer who has just been hired for a specific job, perhaps a cruise line, I want that dancer to be able to pick up this book, look up cruise lines, and in a few moments know:

- What to expect
- What to bring
- How to handle different problems on the ocean

If you are a new dancer leaving for New York or Los Angeles, prepare yourself for all the possibilities of work:

- What type of work are you best suited for
- Who to submit to for an audition
- Understanding your contract

These are questions you'll need answers for. The fact that you are reading this is an important step in preparing yourself.

To write the experiences of all the dancers I have worked with would take volumes and probably lifetimes, but their experiences are invaluable. You can learn some of this important information in your own home town by simply asking around. It sounds easy because it is! Dancers are terrific people and they excel at three things: dancing, eating and TALKING!

Every dancer reading this book should be involved in a dance school, ballet company or high school or college dance program. There is a wealth of experience all around you and they're dying to tell you about it. It's a sure bet that a teacher, owner of a school or possibly another student has a trunk load of information to share. Ask them how they prepared and more importantly, what they were unprepared for. A dance career is different for everyone, so don't be intimidated by the stories of how difficult it is. It _is_ difficult but, if you are trained, talented and hard working, it is possible. Dancers are doing it every day, and you can too!

HAVING THE EDGE

I hear young dancers talking about going to either coast to study. If you are moving to New York or Los Angeles with suitcases and a bank account – GO TO WORK. There is a very different attitude between the studying dancer and the working dancer. It is part competition, maturity and the fact that the rent will not be paid unless you work. You'll be competing with people who want and need work and you will need that same edge going in.

As you look for work, continue to study. It is very important that you learn different styles of choreography and keep your technique sharp. Every class you take and every audition you go to is going to help you accomplish these two endeavors. If you are ready, then take your positive attitude, your dance training and – GO TO WORK!

Finances

How much money do I need to move to the big city? I am asked this question constantly from dancers and actors. My answer is always the same. There is no magic number. I've seen friends go to New York with $600 in their pocket, get a job and make it work. I have also seen friends go with $20,000 in a bank account and come back broke.

But, let's force the issue. If I have to answer the financial question with a specific amount of money, I would say move to New York or Los Angeles with at least $4,000 to $10,000. That may be a wide range for some people, but it does depend on certain elements:

- Non–dancing job skills
- Transportation
- Contacts
- Friends or relatives you can stay with

I've saved this condition for last, because without a doubt, your biggest expense is going to be rent, especially in New York.

I've developed a self–survey to help evaluate your financial readiness. The amount of cash you need can fluctuate, depending on the number of the following questions you can answer YES to:

1. Do I have good non–dancing employment skills?

2. Is there a good possibility I could have some type of income right away?

3. Do I have reliable transportation (for Los Angeles)?

4. Do I know contacts that might help me get work?

5. Do I have someone who might let me stay with them
   for a certain period of time?

Now evaluate your answers. If you can answer yes to four or five of the questions, then it is a good possibility you will need less cash going into New York or Los Angeles than a person answering yes to one or two questions.

This survey is just a <u>guide to start</u> you thinking about your financial readiness. There are many other things to consider:

- Clothes in New York (Especially Winter)
- Pictures and Resumés
- <u>Quality</u> Transportation in L.A.
- Health
- The non–dancing job market is very competitive
- Discipline with money

and many others.

CHAPTER TWO

MEXICO

I interviewed Ron Ruge, choreographer, director and producer with Tiger Productions. Tiger Productions has conceived and produced dozens of shows around the world, including over ten different productions in Mexico City and Acapulco. The interview will give insight into what foreign productions demand, what you are responsible for and a look into the audition.

DM: *Okay, Ron, tell me a little bit about the type of show done abroad and the type of dancer you're looking for.*

RR: First of all, a show cast in LA or Las Vegas for Mexico is almost always a Vegas type revue. Shows may vary as far as style, adding a tap number or an adagio team, but the producers I've worked with always want a bigger than life production. The type of dancer hired is usually the all American blonde glamour type.

DM: *So a blond has an advantage over a brunette and though we'll be talking about the men later, I assume there are many more women hired than men.*

RR: Right! Although I have hired many brunettes, redheads, many Blacks and Asians, the Mexican producers do stress the desire for the all American tall blonde type dancer. However, it is very difficult to cast an entire show with one type; thus, the need for all types of dancers to audition for foreign shows is necessary.

DM: *I've noticed that the younger, less experienced dancer is interested in foreign shows, is that the case?*

RR: Foreign shows are great for the young inexperienced dancer who needs to get stage time and practice their craft. I also see the older dancers who are in great shape, but for some reason can't get work right now in the States. Don't forget it's also great for the dancer who just wants a new adventure or something different.

DM: *When you hire a dancer do they get a contract?*

RR: It depends on the project. I have written contracts in the U.S. to appease the dancer. I feel the dancer should assert themselves if they want a contract, but the truth is contracts in Mexico can be a gamble. You are really depending on the reputation of the Mexican producer.

DM: *A producer the dancer doesn't know.*

RR: Yes. But I know them. I've done many shows in foreign countries and to my knowledge everyone has been paid.

DM: *So you're really the lifeline between the dancer and the Mexican producer.*

RR: Usually the producer does the hiring but because of my earlier experience in Mexico, I try to reassure the dancer. Let me stress, it is the dancers responsibility to find out the legitimacy of the producer and the place you will be working, either by asking around or even asking for a contract and seeing a lawyer. It's really up to you to ask the questions.

DM: *It really is the producer's word, since a dancer would have little recourse against a foreign producer anyway.*

RR: Right. But again, let me say as far as I know, everyone who worked in Mexico has been paid. Remember that this is Mexico, it's a different country. Not to put Mexico down, but you can't expect it to be the United States. The 'mañana' attitude is there in every aspect and though they'll get to the problem, the pace is usually slow.

DM: *Tell me about an audition. What do you want to see and how does the dancer find out about foreign work?*

RR: Basically, you will hear about the auditions in trade papers, the entertainment section of the regular newspaper and especially on a billboard at the local dance studio, and of course, word of mouth. At the audition you have to make an impression right away. Many dancers make the mistake of wearing unattractive dance clothes, little or no makeup, tennis shoes. It's true! In my opinion, do not pull back the hair like ballet class, you should have a full mane. Even if you have short hair, do something chic or glamourous. I would suggest street makeup, but a little on the heavy side, an attractive leotard hiked up to emphasize long legs and DEFINITELY HEELS! I know its not what some dancers want to hear, but in foreign shows, very often, looks are first and dance ability is second.

DM: *What about the men?*

RR: Well, I've had many male dancers go to Mexico, usually to back up a female singing star. The star will ask for four to eight male dancers to perform three or four dance numbers during the course of her act. I have also had male dancers like yourself, perform the lead adagio for a show in Mexico.

DM: *Right.*

RR: Everything for the men is the same. They receive round trip airfare and room. The hotel rooms are always very close to the nightclub in which you work. The only other difference is the female star may travel throughout

Mexico and Spain, and of course, you would travel with it.

DM: *How long do your shows run?*

RR: I've had shows run for two years, but most shows run six to nine months. The dancer will commit to a 6 month obligation with optional three month extensions.

DM: *In your opinion, have the dancers who worked in Mexico enjoyed the trip?*

RR: Yes, but like anything else, some dancers get Montezuma's Revenge the first week, think it's the end of the world and want to go home. Some people can't handle the culture shock. Most dancers have a very satisfying experience, especially those who love to travel and see the sights and meet new people.

DM: *For me, Mexico was great! I was a brand new dancer and it gave me a chance to practice my craft and performance techniques while getting paid and seeing the world.*

RR: Yes, that's exactly how I see it.

WORK

I would like to be very technical and specific in this particular chapter simply because it can mean the difference between a terrific experience and a nightmare. First, always remember you are in a foreign country. Many dancers go to Mexico with the "I'm an American" attitude. This does not work in any country and you would never stand for it if a foreigner did it to you. It is by their grace you're allowed to work in their country.

Secondly, your producer will be responsible for your work visa. As you might remember from the opening story, this is very important. It states simply that you may work in Mexico for a certain amount of time and in a certain capacity. The reason I am saying this is because there is an abundance of work in Mexico for Americans. Though you've heard some negative points, many Mexicans love Americans and like to use them for fashion shows, modeling jobs, choreography and commercials. If you are going to get involved in extra work (and if you can you should), make sure you've discussed it with your producer. The producer is responsible for you while you're working under the work visa they've paid for. They have a right to know if you're moonlighting and may be entitled to some monetary compensation.

Don't be offended if he might feel that way. He may also know of certain restrictions or limitations your work visa might have.   Believe me, the last thing you want to do is break the law in Mexico.

When I worked in Mexico I had the approval of my producer and went on to do many modeling jobs. I even had the chance to choreograph for Televisa, (the equivalent to ABC).   The experience was wonderful and the new people I met added to that experience.   Of course, the extra bucks weren't so bad either.

Now to the show at hand.   Most of your rehearsals will be held in the States for obvious economic reasons, but you will usually get a week of rehearsals on the stage.   The productions are very similar to a Vegas lounge show, they are fast paced flashy dance numbers separating a couple of Mexican variety acts, usually a singer, comedian or magician.

Glitzy costumes, bright lights and a combination of contemporary and Mexican music fill a show rarely longer than two hours in length.   The work week is six nights, one show a night, one day off a week, but can be increased at the producers discretion. ASK AHEAD OF TIME. The show is also a little later than what you might be used to, sometimes starting at 9:00 or 10:00 PM.

I have worked two different nightclubs in Mexico City and one in Acapulco and I've always found them to be just as professional as in the United States.   Remember, the pace is slower and the culture is different.   Stay calm, meet people halfway and keep a professional business attitude and it will ensure a great time.

HELPFUL HINTS

The word for today is passport. Can you say passport?

I knew you could. If you are making dance a career, you need a passport. Now! A passport will cost you about $25 and take a couple of days to process. They are valid for 10 years and when you're hired for a foreign show leaving in five days, you'll be glad you have it.

There is one more thing you need to know about your passport. TREAT IT LIKE GOLD! Keep it with you. You may need to give it to your producer so he can apply for your work visa, but do not let a producer hold the passports of the cast. Demand it back! It's your identification in a foreign country and your right to keep it with you at all times. Am I a little sensitive about this issue? Have I stressed it enough? At the risk of overkill, yes. You see, if I'd had a passport when I went to Mexico, that experience at the beginning of the book would have never happened to me. I never want to see it happen to anyone else.

MONEY

Que dice? Let's talk pesos. Sure, you're going to Mexico to have some fun, perform in a new show and see the country, but it's even more fun if you get to take some of your hard earned money home.

After speaking to two different choreographers about salaries for dancers, I found the salary was the same for over ten different productions, spanning a period of eight years. The salary was $400 a week for chorus, $25 extra for line captain or dance captain and $50 – $100 extra for the leads. In every show except one, the dancers were paid in U.S. dollars. In the one exception, the dancers were paid half in U.S. dollars and half in Mexican pesos.

The importance of being paid in U.S. currency is simply this: when I worked in Mexico City in 1980, the currency exchange was 21 pesos to the U.S. dollar. As of 1993 that exchange rate is 2500 pesos to the U.S. dollar. You can see that there is quite a difference. If you're being paid in U.S. dollars, no matter what the Mexican government does with their currency, your salary won't be affected.

Here's an example of what happened to a very talented adagio team that will help explain the importance of being paid in U.S. dollars. Names and numbers are fictitious, but the story is true. Bill and Sue were hired to dance in Paris, France. They were to perform the lead adagio in a Paris revue and they signed a contract for one year at a certain salary.

Let's say their salary was 1,000 francs a week or the equivalent of $500 a week (remember, I'm making these numbers up to keep it simple and make the point). Six months into the one year contract, the French government devalues their currency due to inflation, economic and political problems. Bill and Sue are still receiving their 1,000 francs a week in accordance with their contract. The difference, is now the U.S. equivalent is only $250. What do you think a salary cut of 50% will have on your morale six months into the run? You're doing the same amount of work, but you're taking home half the money you expected. This is an example of what can happen if you're not careful or you just don't know. When you're about to take work in a foreign country and you're discussing salary, get one of two things in writing.

1. Get paid in U.S. dollars

2. Get paid in the foreign currency in the equivalent of a specified amount of U.S. dollars.

Then no matter what the peso does while you are working in Mexico, you will always be making the same amount in U.S. dollars.

A third option is the one I mentioned earlier, half pesos, half dollars. Again, if the half peso portion remains equivalent to a U.S. dollar amount, then this is a safe compromise. It's also not a bad idea. You're going to need some Mexican currency to live on while you're working in Mexico anyway. Hopefully, you will send the other half home in savings.

Great segue. Send it home. Send your U.S. dollars that you want to save home. Send it home to a bank. Send it home to a parent or trusted friend, but send it home!

Have you ever wondered why the entire world invests their money in America? It's because we have one of the most stable economies in the world. Send it home!

Another horror story. Remember these stories are true and they're the reasons that made me angry enough to carry out this project. Steve (not his real name), is in Acapulco, dancing in a wonderful production. He decides to extend his contract for another six months because he is having such a great time in Acapulco. A Mexican bank is offering 30% interest on a six month certificate of deposit of $5,000 U.S. Steve sees this as a way to make an extra $1,500 in interest in the six months he's going to be in Mexico anyway. Sounds good doesn't it? The problem was the Mexican government devalued the peso over 150% in the six month period and passed a law that no U.S. dollars were to leave the banking system. His guarantee of being paid back in U.S. dollars was now worthless. When Steve got his certificate of deposit in <u>pesos</u>, he found that he had gotten the 30% interest, but the $5,000 U.S. that he had put in the bank had been returned to him in the equivalent of $1,700 U.S. dollars in devalued pesos. $5,000 in, $1,700 out. Send it home!

CREDIT CARDS

Don't leave home without it. No this is not an endorsement for American Express. I really don't care which major credit card you use in the States or whether you're against credit cards all together. When you're working in a foreign country, I strongly recommend having at least one major credit card with you. If you don't have one, try to get one before you leave on your trip. If you do have one, for heavens sake, make sure it's not maxed to its limit (you see, I really do know dancers). The point of having a credit card is not so you can buy more sombreros or silver bracelets, but so you can protect yourself in case anything out of the ordinary happens.

Example: The producers declare bankruptcy, cancel and exchange all your return flight tickets for cash and close the show. I know this is a little dramatic, but it could happen. You don't panic, you don't beat anyone up, you don't have to call Dad. You take your little credit card, book a flight to the States and chalk it all up to experience.

TAXES

Mexico has firmly established what it calls a "luxury" tax. Anything that is not a necessity is a luxury and if you can afford the luxury, you can afford the tax. The tax is 100% on most luxuries, sometimes more. OK, now catch your breath.

When I arrived in Mexico I was surprised to see almost every car on the road was a Volkswagen or an older model American Motors car. When I asked about this my producer explained, "Many other models would be considered luxuries and subject to a 100% tax." I immediately cringed at the thought of possibly being able to afford a new Corvette at $40,000 only to have your dream vanish with the new $80,000 price tag, <u>TAX</u> and license included.

The reason I'm explaining this tax situation is because dancers from foreign countries working in Mexico under work visas fall into this category – "luxuries". Your salary may be the equivalent of $400 U.S. a week, but your producer has had to pay $800 a week in order to assure that you net your contracted amount. "So what," you say. "I don't care what he has to pay as long as I get what I negotiated for." Exactly my point. When I began working other entertainment jobs in Mexico, modeling, television or choreography, I had to ask for double the money I wanted in order to insure that I got paid what I felt the job was worth.

If I felt the job was worth $200, I would ask for $400. One half would come to me and one half to the Mexican Government. I thought you'd like to know. Now remember, tax laws in every country change rapidly and frequently. Ask first.

LIFESTYLE

Mexico City, Acapulco, Cancun, Cozumel or Mazatlan—wherever you travel in Mexico—it's exciting, colorful and very romantic. The festive spirit of the people, restaurants on the beach, mariachis playing, you just can't beat it. Although most dance shows will be performing in Mexico City or Acapulco, a short plane flight can take you almost anywhere in the country. Now before the romantic in me completely takes over, let's talk practically.

COST OF LIVING

I think you will be amazed at how far your money will go in Mexico. Since eighty percent of the American dance shows will be performed in Mexico City, I will use that city as our financial example (remember, tourist cities like Acapulco and Cancun will be more expensive).

Early 1993 the exchange rate is 2,500 pesos to 1 U.S. dollar. I know this doesn't mean anything to many people so let me give you a more personal insight. A dancer in Mexico City will be earning $400 a week, dancing one show a night, six nights a week. When you compare that to the average construction laborer who makes $90 a week U.S. (six days) and has to pay his own rent, you'll begin to see the point. It is my opinion that a dancer can take care of personal items, food, and even entertainment two or three times a week for $100 – $150 U.S. I know this is a base figure, some dancers will spend more, some less, but for those who are trying to save money, you'll be relieved to know that you can enjoy Mexico and still put away $200 – $300 a week.

Example: You can have dinner for two in a fabulous restaurant, mariachis playing, wonderful view of the water, huge seafood platter for two including lobster, shrimp and fish, a couple of margaritas, everything. When the check arrives – around 66,000 pesos or $25 U.S. dollars.

Where do I sign up? I want to go back!

SURVIVING THE CLICHÉS

- Don't drink the water!
- Don't pay the original price – bargain!
- Good Old Montezuma.
- Why don't they speak English?

Just a few of Mexico's good ole clichés. In this section, I'm going to take the last, first, because I feel dealing with the language barrier will solve a multitude of problems. WHY DON'T THEY SPEAK ENGLISH? It never fails, in every dance show there is always one person who is indignant about the fact that more Mexicans don't speak English. It's an arrogance I can hardly tolerate of my fellow Americans.   Can you imagine your attitude if someone from Greece came up to you, asked for directions and became hostile because you didn't speak Greek? Sounds ridiculous doesn't it? Yet many Americans go to Mexico and expect them to speak English. This happens far too often. It's done not just by dancers but by American tourists. You can hear them yelling in the marketplace because some poor Mexican is only smart enough to speak the language of his native country. When the truth is, it's our fault for not preparing ourselves to visit this foreign country. The solution is very simple.

When you're hired to dance in Mexico, do your best to learn the language. As soon as possible, buy a book or tape and take them with you.

You don't have to be a whiz with languages to be able to communicate basic needs. The difference in the way you'll be treated is enormous. Most Mexicans are good natured, good hearted people. When you make an <u>attempt</u> to speak with them in their language they will usually laugh, and then go out of their way to help you. I literally had people inviting me to their homes for dinner and to meet their families. I wouldn't recommend this to everyone, especially for female dancers, but it is fun to make friends of different cultures and attempting to speak Spanish is the best way to break the ice.

Since I had a six month contract to work in Mexico City, I hired a tutor to teach me Spanish. Berlitz is a wonderful, well known language school but very expensive. In search of another alternative, I looked in the phone book (they have some in English in the hotel). I found many reputable schools including one offering private lessons twice a week, 3 hours per day, for $17 U.S. a month. Such a deal!

It is truly worth the money when you consider how fast you can learn the language. You see, everything you learn in class you can immediately apply. Soon the other dancers were calling on me to order for them in a restaurant or bargain at the market. More importantly, having just a slight command of the language allowed me to get a lot of extra work in dance because I could express my desire to choreograph or be part of another production.

BARGAINING AT THE MARKET

Once you get the hang of this you'll wonder why we don't do more bargaining here in the States. It does take some getting used to. I found myself bargaining from one extreme to the other. At first, I was a little self conscious and felt uncomfortable trying to get an item at a cheaper price, but once I got the hang of it I would try to get everything for free! Bargaining prices in Mexico is as socially accepted as our handshake and a lot more fun. You'll be surprised to see vendors reduce their initial price 50 – 80%. Soon the shopping stories start, "He wanted this much, but I told him I would only pay this much." Everyone tells their friends what a great shopper they are, but the truth is the vendor wouldn't sell it if he didn't make a profit.

One of the best ways to approach bargaining for a specific item is to decide how much you would honestly pay for the item (on sale of course) and try to talk the vendor down to that price. Then everyone is happy and you can go home and say, "Well, he wanted $40 for it but I got it for $10."

Important note: You can not bargain for certain things. The prices in the menu of a fine restaurant are not up for negotiating, but very often you can negotiate the price of a ride in a taxi. The important thing in negotiating the price of a cab is to do all your bargaining before you get in. Once you are in the cab, the price is no longer negotiable.

DON'T DRINK THE WATER

The oldest and most talked about cliché concerning Mexico. They seem inseparable. You can't mention going to Mexico without someone saying "Don't drink the water." The truth is many dancers and tourists have been fine after drinking water in restaurants and nightclubs. Upscale resorts boast about their purified water, but Montezuma has put the fear of God into us Yankees and until Mexico has a national purification system, I can't recommend drinking anything but bottled water. Bottled water is inexpensive and available everywhere in Mexico.

So here is a cliché that will remain for awhile. Remember, it's not just water in its simplest form, but ordering a soft drink with ice is also a main concern. Fruits, raw vegetables and salads rinsed with water have been known to cause an uncomfortable day or two.

The first time I danced in Mexico, I was sick on three different occasions. Of course, I never ate in the hotel, I was always venturing out, eating everywhere and anywhere. Well, when you are doing a fast paced dance show at night with no understudies you cannot afford to be sick. Again, being able to speak a little Spanish saved the day. I ran into a "farmacia" and asked the pharmacist what would help. He showed me a special type of Pepto–Bismol with neomycin. Neomycin is an antibiotic that evidently has an effect on the bacteria that causes us so much trouble. I can't say that it's for everyone, but I was feeling great in about two hours. Ask your doctor or pharmacist before you leave for Mexico if there is anything new on the market that might help.

PRECAUTIONS

This is a difficult section, but one I will repeat throughout the book. Mexico City is as large or larger than Los Angeles, and like most cities has the same crime problems. You should always be conscious of this. A great characteristic of a dance show is the cast usually gets very close and enjoys sightseeing and partying together. If this happens to your cast, great, but for some reason if you do venture out alone, make sure someone knows where you went and approximately what time you will return. The female dancers in my cast would either ask one of the male dancers to go with them or the girls would go out together and take their umbrellas with them. This was a great idea, since it rains frequently and unexpectedly they didn't look out of place and their umbrellas could double as protection in case of an emergency.

Another major precaution is against fire. Whenever you are staying in a new unfamiliar place such as a hotel, KNOW YOUR FIRE EXITS WELL. It may seem silly, but you should be able to find the nearest exit with your eyes closed, even on your hands and knees. You see, even if the fire is not serious, the smoke may be too thick to see. Count the number of doors down the hall to the exit and know more than one exit. Another hint is to try to request a room on the lowest floor as possible. I'll tell you why.

I was staying at the beautiful Fiesta Palace Hotel. I had been there about three weeks when early one morning a maid came barging into my room screaming something in Spanish. Now although I speak Spanish, I do not wake up in Spanish.

Confusion in these situations can be a killer. I finally realized that she was yelling 'fire', and since my room was full of smoke, I believed her. I had to find the stairway with my eyes almost closed and run down twenty-four flights of stairs in a bathrobe. Not a good way to start the day.

I found out later that the air conditioner had caught fire and although the fire was immediately contained, it filled the rooms with smoke. I was glad to know where the fire exits were. When traveling, take your fire precautions seriously.

SIGHTSEEING

Only one thing to say about sightseeing in Mexico, DO IT! Every trip I made was wonderful. The pyramids, parks, museums, botanical gardens, beaches, nightclubs, shopping, everything. Mexico has a very modern subway system similar to Paris and light years ahead of New York. Although it is very crowded, it is easy to negotiate around town and very inexpensive. We're talking pennies here.

Another adventure in sightseeing is to rent a Volkswagen and experiment on your own. The hotels do carry maps in English and the tourist spots are accentuated. Remember to purchase car insurance. Your U.S. car insurance is not valid there. One other thing, when you are driving your rented car, be sure to beep your horn a lot. I don't know why, but it doesn't seem to have the hostile connotations it does in the States. So beep your horn, smile, and maybe someone will think you are a local.

CLASS

Yes, you can take class in Mexico. And what a trip! They love to use American music to teach class, so you will probably recognize the tune but not the words as they'll be in Spanish. This will keep you laughing through most of the class. If that wasn't enough, the chance of your instructor speaking English is very slim. Fortunately, dance is very physical and visual, because it really is a kick to get all your choreography and corrections in a foreign language and still make it happen. Keep laughing, the teacher and other students will have as much fun with this as you will.

The truth is most Americans with any dance training at all can teach jazz in Mexico. The quality of jazz dance is really behind the times. So get a good stretch, keep in shape and have some fun, but don't expect to pick up too many new steps or styles. The price of class is very reasonable, slightly lower than what you might pay in the States. I have visited quite a few schools in Mexico City, but haven't seen many schools outside of the city. If you have the chance to teach you should go for it. Let me tell you all you'll need to know; uno, dos, tres, quatro, cinco, seise, siete, ocho. Everything else is universal.

CHAPTER THREE

JAPAN

Needing an expert on Japanese productions, I interviewed Minnie Madden. Throughout Tokyo and rural Japan, Minnie has choreographed twelve different productions. She has also produced and directed nine other shows.

DM: *Briefly tell me about the type of show done in Japan.*

MM: I've hired anywhere from 6 to 16 dancers for a particular show, so the Japanese shows range from a small lounge show to a small production show. Because of the language barrier we use an incredibly large volume of dance. You see, everything must be visual, even the acts I hire will be visual acts; jugglers, magicians for example. Obviously no American comedians, only visual acts.

DM: *I've heard the difference between a show in Tokyo and a show in rural Japan is night and day?*

MM: Night and day, totally night and day. Tokyo is a major city, the money for dancers is better, the facilities are better, the production values are better. The buyers in Tokyo are major buyers. You don't have to sell them on the show, they want the show and they know what they're doing. Outside of Tokyo we jokingly call the boonies. One dancer to another we say the show is out in the boonies or country. The show is on a much smaller scale. Although the people are just as nice, they can't charge their public as much as the city and they can't afford the large production values but more importantly, they can't pay the dancers as much.

DM: *Where do you cast?*

MM: Mainly in Las Vegas, sometimes in LA. An experienced dancer who has gone to Japan before will submit their picture and resumé to me if they want to do another show in Japan.

DM: *I understand that the producer from Japan is looking for a certain type of dancer, not always your choice but their choice.*

MM: Right! This is unfortunate, but their greatest interest is in youth. If I'm producing for Japan I can get myself in trouble if I hire someone who's 33 years old even if they're wonderful at what they do and look great. I'm not kidding, they check the passports.

DM: *Really!*

MM: They just have a thing about age. As an American it's shocking because we're into excellence and the talent of a dancer and would much rather have the experience and the veteran performance that an 18 year old can't possibly have.

DM: *Same for men?*

MM: Men, it doesn't matter. No, their age doesn't matter, their height doesn't matter. They just want the show to have an American look. It isn't prejudice, it's the show they're buying. When they purchase a British show or a Chinese show, they want that look. When they hire a French Revue, they want the dancers to be French looking. Don't misunderstand, I've never had any problem hiring blacks or Hispanics, they just want a clean–cut American look. I'm glad about this because if they didn't, I don't think I would take the contract because that kind of thinking is unacceptable to me.

DM: *OK, back to the type of show. Fast moving, glitz, lights, heavy dancing, what else?*

MM: Heavy dancing! OK, lets do Tokyo versus the boonies, what we'll call the boonies. In the boonies they want the look to be more important than the show. They want the young, tall, very pretty, boobs and feathers show, even if it's not topless. When they think of a Vegas revue they think boobs and feathers. In Tokyo this is not true. In Tokyo, you can do much more contemporary things, much more street dancing. They don't care about the feathers and all that stuff. They live in a contemporary city, they've seen more and they want good hot dancing.

DM: *Audition time! I'm a dancer going to your call, I want to wear the right thing, I want to look the right way and I want to know what you expect of me.*

MM: Let's take the men, that's simple. You should show up in jazz shoes, jazz pants, not jeans! I've seen guys show up in jeans a lot. Even if you can stretch in them, it just gives off an attitude like you don't care. For girls, I think it's important that they wear character heels but bring flats. There are many styles of dance, some of which are better performed in flats, so whether it's tennis shoes or jazz shoes, bring them.

DM: *What about hair and makeup?*

MM: I don't think women need stage makeup at an audition, just full makeup, or what I call TV makeup. Don't assume the producer knows what you'll look like on stage. So many times the agent and the hotel owner will be at the audition and will have the final say on who's hired. I've been at auditions where producers from Japan picked girls who were less attractive, but were in full makeup wearing nice leotards, fishnets and heels. Other girls wore light makeup and jazz pants that didn't show the body. The latter girls were stronger dancers and prettier, but they weren't made up and didn't get the job. I remember this vividly because they all had this look of shock on their face. You see, dancers make the mistake of assuming everyone has a dancer's perspective. Entertainment buyers and agents don't have a dancer's perspective and the Japanese <u>definitely</u> don't have a dancer's perspective.

DM: *It's strange that dance is the last thing thought about at the audition, but let's get to it. What about dance?*

MM: <u>Strong</u>! Strong jazz – almost all jazz. Every once in a while a tap number will be put in but almost entirely jazz.   Let me stress something else. SELL. You must sell the audition. Though I have a lot of say in who's hired, the producers from Japan will always have the final word and they will always choose the smiling and selling dancer over the moody artistic one. They don't buy that. I will teach the combination until you get it. I'm not big on a dancer having to have the combination in 5 minutes.   I know you're nervous and I know you'll do better in a rehearsal. To me, picking up the combination fast is not a good judge of dance ability.

DM: *Minnie, what about contracts and payment?*

MM: Everyone gets a contract stating basically dates, money and work expected of you. You'll be paid in U.S. dollars, receive transportation, room and board.   In 19 productions, everyone has always been paid.

The agents I've worked with in Japan are reputable. My people always get paid and that's the reputation I want.

Minnie Madden has a wealth of knowledge about working in Japan. Her point of view is not just as the producer. Being a dancer she is always conscious of the needs of dancers. She had many other things to say in our interview that I will edit and relay under the categories of Work, Money and Lifestyle.

WORK

Going to Japan? Take your stamina with you because if you've accepted a job in Japan be prepared to work. Most shows are seven days a week. You will usually perform three shows a day and you might be able to get one day off a month. Frightening, isn't it? The shows run an hour to an hour and fifteen minutes with two or three acts, but they are fast paced, hard dancing shows. Your rehearsal period will be in two stages. First, a two to three week session in the states where the show will be choreographed and staged. Then, you will travel to Japan and have two or three days on stage to acclimate lights and sound.

Let me summarize by giving two examples of six month contracts in Japan. Outside Tokyo the same show will run two to six months, and although you're dancing three shows a day, your rehearsal schedule will be minimal because you're performing the same show. You can expect some brush up or clean up rehearsals. Again, if the attendance is down sometime during the run you may get a day off.

In Tokyo, a show will run for thirty days and will be replaced by a new show every thirty days. Now, you have a six month contract, performing three shows a day, seven days a week for thirty days. If that's not hard enough, you will also be rehearsing next months show sometime during the day. I can hear you moaning! I'm sure you're dying to find out about the money (next section). I'm not kidding when I say Japan is a work oriented country.

On the bright side, I've talked with many dancers who have worked in Japan and were glad they went. Minnie Madden estimated that out of a hundred people hired for Japan, 90–95% have enjoyed it and would go again.

WORK VISAS

You'll of course need a passport for Japan. You will need to relinquish it <u>temporarily</u> to the Japanese Embassy to stamp it and validate your work visa. Like the U.S., the laws on work visas change constantly and keeping up is difficult, but as of this writing the agent in Japan is responsible for your work visa. The visa is valid for six months and no longer. With this particular work visa you are allowed to moonlight in the dance or modeling field, although I can't imagine where you'd find the time or energy.

QUESTION YOUR PRODUCER

Remember, your producer in the States is your lifeline of information. <u>Ask all the questions you can.</u> Where are you performing? What part of the country? Where are you living? Have they seen it? How many shows a day? How many different shows in the run?   How much money in U.S. dollars? Minnie Madden has agreed that most producers will tell the truth, good or bad. A producer doesn't want an irritable unhappy dancer in a foreign country. It just means more work for them. You see, if a producer lies to a dancer about the job, it makes it more difficult to find quality dancers to do their next show. It's good business for a producer to tell the truth and it's good business for you to ask all the questions you possibly can before accepting a job in Japan.

HOSTESSING

Hostessing has always had a shady, uneasy connotation to it. I think it's because the definition is so vague. It can mean anything from seating people in a restaurant, to social dancing, to prostitution, which leads to white slavery! Oh my God! The young girl went to Japan, they stole her passport, she can't get away and they've forced her into a life of sexual slavery. I think they made a TV Movie of the Week out of that story. I'm sure it did happen somewhere, sometime, but not to dancers performing lounge shows in Japan.

Hostessing may be part of your work commitment. ASK! Find out what is expected of you before and after the show. Japan places a high priority on being polite, courteous and social. Men, women and entire families will want to talk with you, learn things about America and tell you about themselves. It's very important in their culture to be extremely social and hospitable hosts while you're in their country. It's also very prestigious to be seen out on the town with Americans, but don't misunderstand, they are sincere. They may buy you a drink, dinner or give a small gift and expect nothing in return but social grace and good company.

Japan is fascinating in that everything has its place. If a Japanese man is interested in a sensual evening, there's a place for that. There are baths and geisha girls everywhere. If he is interested in a pleasant evening of conversation with a foreigner, that too has its special place. I know this is strange to our way of thinking. Here is one of my true example stories that might help.

Susan was dancing in a Tokyo production and one night decided to have a drink after the show with a couple of friends of the producer. She talked with one man in particular for about two hours. The next evening they talked again. They laughed about his broken English, the differences in cultures and were becoming friends. Only at the end of this evening the Japanese man gave Susan a very beautiful watch as a gift. Well, immediately all the warning lights went off in Susan's head. She refused the gift, but when the Japanese man kept insisting, she courteously accepted. Susan was feeling very uncomfortable now and was looking for any excuse to escape. The young man must have sensed her anxiety because the next evening, he met with the producer, called Susan in and gave her another gift. This time he brought his wife and entire family with him. The gesture was to sincerely thank her for being his friend and bringing his family was to prove to her that his intentions were honorable.

You may be asked to hostess between shows or after the show. Find out before you accept the job.

MONEY

Income does not always mean cold hard cash. You must look at the benefits offered with the cash in order to complete the picture. Here's a comparison example.

In Mexico City the average American dancer can eat very well, very cheaply. Entertainment is also relatively inexpensive, so when a producer in Mexico offers $400 a week and a hotel room, that's not such a bad deal. In Tokyo, one of the most expensive cities in the world, that won't cut it. The Japanese producers adapt this way. Most jobs going to Japan will pay $350 – $450 U.S. dollars a week, but they will enhance your income by paying for your room and board. Board will include two meals a day. Everyone I talked with felt there was always good food available and plenty of it. In any other country, you might say, "So what! I'll pay for my own food and eat what I like." In any other country you might be right, but Japan is home to the $7 cup of coffee, $15 beer and $13 ham sandwich. Board can be the most important benefit negotiated in your contact. In fact, if board is not offered as part of your compensation for working in Japan, I would strongly suggest not taking the job. Without board, you will spend almost your total salary just to eat. In Japan, a quarter–pounder with cheese at McDonald's is just over $10.

Another incredible benefit while working Japan is medical coverage. Hotels and nightclubs are bonded medically for all employees, <u>this includes you</u>. I know of dancers who have injured themselves on the job. They were immediately taken to the hospital, treated and escorted home. All costs, medications, and transportation expenses for follow up care were covered. There was even compensation while injured or ill. When you consider how few non–union dance jobs have any type of medical coverage, this is quite a plus. I want to make you aware of how invaluable some benefits can be.

LIFESTYLE

To enjoy Japan it might help if you know a little history and even a little geography. RELAX! I'll keep it short. Japan is a lovely land with magnificent mountain ranges principally due to it's volcanic origin. Japan is densely populated with over 120 million people, 12 million living in Tokyo alone. There are four major islands, Honshu, Kyushu, Hokkaido and Shikoku. Three quarters of the entire population live on the main island of Honshu. The major cities on this island are Tokyo, Yokohama, Kyoto, Kobe, Osaka and Nagoya. These cities are modern, sophisticated and crowded. Japan's population is sixth in the world. That's 120 million people in an area about the size of Montana.

Even though Japan cannot feed itself fully, it has the distinction of producing more food per acre than any other country. Japan boasts the world's largest fishing fleet, nearly one-half million boats. Understandably, fish replaces meat in most dishes. Meat prices are staggering!

CLIMATE

The United States and Japan have about the same latitudes and the climate can be compared to our east coast from Florida to Maine. The average temperature in Tokyo is about 57 degrees, but will go below freezing in winter and into the 90's in summer. Like Washington D.C., Tokyo is very humid and much like New York City the coldest month is February and the hottest is August. May and June can be considered the rainy season and it may rain for 30 consecutive days during this time. Surprisingly, Tokyo receives twice as much rainfall as London. Tokyo's summer is damp and hot, autumn is lovely and winter is cold with bright sunshine. The variety of climate in Japan is what's so incredible. In the mountains just outside of Tokyo, there are many ski resorts and plenty of snow, yet in the valleys below they will be growing oranges at the same time.

CURRENCY

The unit of currency in Japan is the Yen, (¥). Bills are 500, 1000, 5000 and 10,000 Yen. Coins are 1, 5, 10, 50, 100 and 500 Yen. Since 1971, by agreement with the United States and Japan the Yen has been allowed to float. The exchange rate from dollars to Yen changes constantly.

TRAVEL

Getting a taxi in the business or entertainment areas is never easy and at rush hour or in the rain, practically impossible. Try to order a cab ahead of time. Taxis can usually be found more easily at hotels and taxi stands. Japanese taxis display a red light on the left side of the windshield when empty and a green light when occupied. Passengers usually ride in the back unless there are too many to squeeze in. The back doors of the cab are opened and closed automatically by the driver so remember to stay clear. Whenever in a taxi, make a habit of taking one of the taxi company business cards with the driver's name and number. This way, if there's any trouble or if you leave something in the cab, it can be easily traced.

Very few taxi drivers in Japan speak English, so either practice the pronunciation of your destination or have someone write it down for you in Japanese. Also, major Japanese cities are large and dense so unless your destination is a well known place you may have to give directions.

Pay the fare shown on the meter when you arrive at your destination before you get out of the taxi. A surcharge is added between the hours of 11 PM and 5 AM or if you ordered the taxi by telephone. No tip is needed.

SUBWAYS

Tokyo, Osaka and Nagoya all have safe and clean subway systems. This is a highly developed public transport system that is convenient and inexpensive. The subway station entrances are usually marked in Japanese and English. On the first floor you will find ticket offices, fare maps, fare machines and the ticket barrier leading downstairs to the second floor and subway platform.

First, locate where you are and where you want to go on the fare map. Right below your destination will be the cost of your subway ride. Now, don't be intimidated by the fare machines since most tickets for subways and local trains are purchased here.

Check the fare to your destination, put the money in the slot, press the appropriate fare button and take the ticket and change. Most ticket machines accept coins only, but some will take 1,000 ¥ bills. If you need change ask at the ticket office or at the ticket barrier. Next, take your ticket to the ticket barrier, an inspector will punch your ticket as you enter (Kaisatsu) and collect it as you leave at your destination (Shussatsu). If you see an automatic ticket gate, slide your ticket in the slot walk forward to the other end, take your ticket from the second slot and the gate will open automatically. You may be nervous and confused at first, but once you get used to using the subway system, it really is the best way to get around.

MAIL

You can find English speaking personnel at the customs office and at most International Post Offices. They are open from 8 AM to 8 PM. Stamps may be bought at hotels, post offices and at any small shop that displays a red and white double capped T. Red postboxes are for ordinary mail, blue ones for 'express' mail or special delivery. In Tokyo if there are two slots on the red box, the right–hand one is for Tokyo, left for everywhere else.

Air mail to the USA or Europe will take six to nine days.

CREDIT CARDS, TRAVELERS CHECKS

All major credit cards and travelers checks are accepted in the larger establishments. American Express, for example, is accepted in over 3,200 establishments. Most of the western style hotels and shops will exchange travelers checks, U.S. dollars and pounds sterling. The use of personal checks or cashier checks is not advised as it is time consuming (clearance can take up to three weeks) and involves much red tape.

TIPPING

A charming courtesy in Japan is that you never slip money to anyone without first wrapping it in something, a paper napkin, a bit of paper, an envelope. This includes tips to waitresses, doormen or bellhops. Never try to tip someone who has given you directions or done a kindness, they would feel insulted, just thank them warmly.

Sidewalk shoe shine boys build in their own tips by charging foreigners more than they do Japanese. Don't give them more than they ask.

SHOPPING

Let's talk about something I know most of you take seriously. Shopping! Here are some of the main department stores, Matsuya, Mitsukoshi, Matsuzakaya. All stores are open on Sunday in Japan. This is the big shopping day. Hours for business are similar to ours, large stores are open 10

AM to 6 PM and small shops are often open till 10 PM. When buying clothes in a regular Japanese department store, be prepared for the fact that sizes come in small, medium and large. That's it! Don't be in a hurry. Shopping in Japan is a casual leisure sport. Even the smallest packages are slowly, carefully and beautifully wrapped. Be prepared to pay in cash more than you are accustomed to doing. Only the larger stores have charge accounts. When you enter Japan, be sure to get a "Record of Purchases of Commodities Tax Exempt for Export" form from the Customs Office. Take this form with you when you make a major purchase. If you don't you may have to pay a heavy fee when you leave the country.

PACKING LIST

Minnie Madden has prepared a packing list that is given to every cast member prior to leaving for Japan. Look over the list. Some things to think about. Fishnets and nylons for tall women are difficult if not impossible to find in Japan. Bring extra! A towel in Japan is a little larger than our washcloth. You might need four towels to dry off. Bring your own!

Suggested Packing List
    Dance Shoes
    Character (1) (plus backup if available)
    Jazz Shoes
    Fishnets (suntan 2 pair)
    Rehearsal Wear
    Personal G—string(s)
    Stage Makeup (lashes)
    Hair equipment (pins, spray, rubber bands, etc.)

    <u>Toiletries</u>
    Towel/Washcloth
    Laundry Soap
    Iron (1 per group)
    Alarm Clock
    Tapes/Recorder
    Books/Magazines/Stationery
    Pajamas/Slipper/Robe
    Comfortable shoes (easy to take off and put on)
    Umbrella
    Hat/Gloves/Scarf
    Sweater(s)
    Jacket
    1—2 Evening Wear (dress)
    Warm comfortable clothes
    Camera/Battery/Film
    Optional
    Scissors, tape
    Aspirin/Midol
    Sewing Kit
    Dramamine/Gum (for plane)

CLASS

Like everything else, class in Japan is intense! It's very competitive, not only for the dancer, but between schools.

There are four major dance schools in Tokyo:

Broadway Dance Center

Ichi Bunga

Professional Dance Center

IBC

These studios are always competing to be the best school with the best teachers, facilities and stereo equipment. One of the reasons the schools are so competitive is because they sell memberships to their dancers. It's the same way we might join a health club or a country club.

Dancers are loyal to one studio, paying a membership fee for a year. Membership fees are expensive, but don't worry, a visiting dancer is able to pay for one class at a time. The individual class fee is usually around $20. This is a little higher than what we're used to paying, but many schools give discounts to American dancers working in their country.

Let me tell you one reason classes in Japan are so expensive. The competition between major schools is so great, they'll pay well known American teacher/choreographers top dollar to teach at their school.

Jaymi Marshall, an excellent choreographer and a good friend is paid $1700 a week to teach one or two classes a day. This is far more than he could make in the states. Jaymi told me the major schools have at least one well known American teacher working for them at any given time.   Some American teacher/choreographers go to Japan once or twice a year for 4 to 6 weeks at a time. Now, don't get me wrong. Unlike Mexico, the Japanese teachers are qualified, up to date and able to teach you new styles and steps. The Japanese dancers are also capable of performing on the same level as American dancers. Japanese studios are complete, offering jazz, ballet, tap, hip hop, traditional Japanese dances, everything. You can consider taking class in Japan a <u>plus</u> if you're going there to work.

CHAPTER FOUR

THEME PARKS

DISNEY

Disney is a major employer of dancers and is getting bigger all the time. I spoke with John Anello, Manager of Talent Resources for the west coast. Ronny Rodrigues is casting manager for the Florida properties. Because LA is so large with an enormous pool of dancers, John will cast almost exclusively in LA. Ronny Rodrigues will cast in Florida, but mostly travels around the country in search of dancers, dancer–singers, singers and masters of ceremony. John gave me a few examples of how dancers are utilized in all Disney properties. <u>Parade dancers</u>; dancers and characters hired for specialty parades. <u>Special productions</u>; shows like "Beauty and the Beast", at Videopolis that will have limited runs. Finally, an example like "Golden Horseshoe" that are staples of the park and will most likely run forever. Disney is very protective of their image. Getting information from Disney was difficult and they remain vague on a variety of topics but here's what they did say.

DM: *I don't think dancers are aware of how many dancers Disney hires.*

JA: That may be true. It's an interesting thing. We advertise in all LA trade papers and Ronny will tour the country to cast for the three Florida properties.

DM: *What are some of the differences?*

JA: Well, I really can't speak for Ronny, but because they bring people to Florida from other areas, they usually have a year contract. In LA, I do a lot more short term projects and one shot deals, except for our stage productions.

DM: *I remember shows like the "Golden Horseshoe" using dancers.*

JA: Right! "Golden Horseshoe" in LA, "Diamond Horseshoe" in Florida. In those shows we have horseshoe dancers, can–can dancers and the guy dancers are cowboys. This is a long term production.

DM: *Different for parade dancers?*

JA: Yes, parade dancers are a whole different level of dancer and fill a different requirement. I don't hire parade dancers, that's another department. But, very often, a parade dancer that has been with us awhile will move up into one of our productions.

DM: *Tell me about the production shows.*

JA: The ongoing shows like the "Golden Horseshoe" run five days a week.

DM: *More in the summer?*

JA: No, probably not. I think it will remain five days a week, five shows a day, as of right now. The show we're running presently at Videopolis is "Beauty and the Beast". It opened in February and will probably run till the end of the summer. We've been running only weekends, but recently went to seven days. We'll keep it seven days a week through the summer. At this point, we don't know if we'll continue with "Beauty and the Beast" or not, so neither do the dancers. That's one of the problems with limited runs.

DM: *How many dancers are in "Beauty and the Beast"?*

JA: Approximately 8–10 dancers in the show plus substitutes in case someone is sick or hurt.

DM: *Is it like the film?*

JA: It's loosely based on the film. It's heavily costumed, in fact, it's a very full production. Costumes, lighting, music written for the show, scenery, everything.

DM: *A big production. Are the dancers costumed as characters, you know, like the tea cup or the candle or is my image wrong.*

JA: Very rarely, the dancers are in crowd scenes as townspeople or ballroom couples. They are the glue that moves the show along. It's a mix. Many of our shows are a mix of dancers, characters and principal roles.

DM: *How long is the show?*

JA: Our shows are 25 minutes.

DM: *Will they sing?*

JA: When we audition, we'll almost always ask dancers to sing. In this particular show they'll just dance.

DM: *What will a dancer make for this type of show?*

JA: I can't tell you that.

DM: *All right then. Tell me what you look for in a dancer.*

JA: We have an audition coming up for a tour that's going around the country. It's called the Symphonic Fantasy Tour. We'll be casting 18 dancers. Now every time we cast a show, the requirements for the dancers change. When we did "Beauty and the Beast" some of the dancers had to have strong ballet training, others had to have a strong tap and jazz background. Now the Symphonic Tour we're sending out will have to have strong ballet dancers including point work. The advice we give to people is they need to do it all. They should constantly be in dance class. The frustration we have in casting is many times a dancer has a certain strength in one area, but not in another. What makes a dancer valuable to us is versatility. For our purposes, the choreographer needs to feel no matter what they come up with to make a show work, the people they've hired will be able to pull it off. A dancer's strength is versatility.

DM: *What's the rehearsal period?*

JD: Well, generally speaking a rehearsal period is two to three weeks. Rehearsals will be local or at the park.

DM: *I know you can't give me figures, but rehearsal pay is different from show pay?*

JA: Yes. If you contact AGVA (The American Guild of Variety Artists) you can find out what the going rates are.

DM: *Then Disney follows AGVA minimums?*

JA: Well, every park cuts their own deals. I'm just in no position to talk money. All I can say is there's a rate for rehearsals and a rate for performance.

DM: *Are dancers hired by Disney, employees of Disney or are they sometimes hired by a production company?*

JA: Dancers working in the park will be Disney employees while they are working. We don't sub–contract shows to independent production companies in the park.

DM: *The Symphonic Tour will be the same thing?*

JA: The hiring process may be different. If they've hired outside the park it may not always be AGVA.

DM: *What about benefits?*

JA: Depends on time worked. You have to have a certain number of hours per week and a certain number of weeks worked. There are all kinds of levels. They have numbers like 02, 03. Depending on time, each one of those levels dictates the amount of coverage they get.

DM: *So a dancer is rewarded for long term employment?*

JA: Yes. The dancers at the "Horseshoe" tend to be involved longer than "Beauty and The Beast" and other shows. They would accumulate benefits.

DM: *Any type of height requirements or ethnic background.*

JA: No, never, if they're good, they're good! We hire everybody.

DM: *Anything else about the audition process you'd like to see.*

JA: I like to see a dancer come prepared. If you are asked to sing, bring an up–tempo and a ballad. Dress comfortably, but dress so it shows you at your best. We will set up the audition out of this office. A choreographer, show director, my casting assistant and myself will hold the call. The thing dancers must know, they get one shot to show what they can do. They should take inventory of themselves. Be smart! Be realistic, and say, "What is it I can show these people, that will make them feel they need to have me in their show." Studying, practicing and being prepared!   You need to tell them to continually take dance class. They better start learning to sing also because more and more we need both. When we hire, the difference between the one we hire and the one we didn't may be their ability to sing.

DM: What about picture and resumé?

JA: They should <u>always</u> have a good, current picture and resumé.   We do consider it because we want to see their experience. That doesn't mean if they don't have experience they won't be hired. We just hired a girl fresh out of school. It just happened that she came in and blew us away. She was well trained and well prepared.

DM: Do you hire in LA for parks in Paris and Japan?

JA: Actually, there's a tour that goes around the country every six months to find talent for Japan. Ronny Rodrigues does that tour with a choreographer and a show director from Japan. They make the decisions and we make all the job offers from this office.

   John Anello was very helpful in letting us know what Disney's needs are in terms of dance. They're a little secretive in terms of money, but that's their prerogative.   Not everyone is comfortable talking about money. I did contact AGVA. They told me they do have contracts with Disney. In fact, they have contracts with Universal and Six Flags (covered next). Disney does adhere to AGVA minimums in the theme park.

I can't tell you exactly what you'll make working the "Golden Horseshoe" but AGVA minimums are $670 per five day week for dancers and $793 per five day week for principal roles. AGVA also has medical benefits for dancers after a certain amount of work is performed. At Disney, this period is 15 days in one show. After 15 days, Disney will begin to contribute to your insurance premiums. This changes frequently from park to park. Universal will begin paying into your benefits after six months! Disney should be considered as a good and major employer of dancers. You can stay in one park or tour. You can have long term employment or audition for a limited run. Many dancers in LA work Disney and audition for other jobs. So take John's advice. Be prepared and give it your best shot. Watch for audition notices in trades or your local newspaper. If you'd like to submit to Disney, send a picture and a resumé to:

Talent Booking
Disney Entertainment
P.O. Box 3232
Anaheim, CA 92803

UNIVERSAL STUDIOS

Universal Studios Theme Park is so exciting I'm throwing away my interview format and giving you the information straight out. I did speak with Don Burgess, Entertainment Director of Universal Studios Co. and he made it clear, "This is a wonderful opportunity for a dancer." Currently, there are seven entertainment shows using dancers. Seven! No other employer encourages and rewards the versatile dancer like Universal Studios. I'm talking about the dancer who sings, the dancer who acts, and the dancer with the ability to do stunts.

Here is a quick breakdown of shows currently performed:

The Blues Brothers	Dancing and singing
Doo Wop	Dancing and singing
An American Tail	Costumed characters dancing, no vocals, tap, jazz, working with animation
Beetlejuice	Hip Hop, Jazz, rock vocals, heavy makeup
Conan	Choreographed sword fights, acting
Riot Act	Acting and stunts
Miami Vice	Acting and stunts

As you can see, there's something for everyone. There's a reason I'm including stunt shows. Many dancers, male and female, were hired initially for a particular dance show and over time expressed interest in and showed ability to perform stunts. Don Burgess informed me there are dancers in every show at Universal Theme Park. This is just one example of how Universal Studios encourages the ambitious dancer and gives them the opportunity to increase their salary and their value as a well rounded dancer.

Universal utilizes a stepladder system. Each of the seven shows previously mentioned has 6 or 7 separate casts. When you're hired, you may be placed in cast 6 or cast 7 and as you train, perform and gain experience you'll move up to cast 1–3. This is very important since it is only casts number 1–3 that receive total health care benefits not to mention priority with scheduling and days off. This may initially sound harsh, but again it does encourage and reward long term employment.

For the exceptionally talented dancer they do allow crossover. This is where a dancer will learn more than one show and perform different shows during the course of the day. This is another way to earn more money and increase your value to your employer. These crossover dancers are also very important in the case of an injury or other emergency and are jokingly called "the fire brigade".

Consider this! Universal Studios Theme Park will give a dancer time off to perform other jobs in the industry. This is unheard of in the dance world! Of course, the outside work must be approved by

Universal and your time off is without pay, but your job will be secure until you return from your other dance job. This is great! While you're working at Universal you can audition for other dance jobs. Example... Say you land a job dancing on the Academy Awards Special. You'll be allowed to rehearse, perform the special, work for a new choreographer, make money, gain experience and return to a full time job right away.

Don Burgess said, "We want a long term dancer, a happy dancer and an experienced dancer and we think it's important to allow a dancer to gain that experience and bring it back to Universal." This is a plus you can't put a monetary value on.

ABOUT THE WORK

With many dance jobs you may work for a subcontracted production company (see Six Flags Magic Mountain), but with Universal you become a Universal employee and receive the benefits all Universal employees receive. Although park rules are standard for each show, contracts are different for each show. I wasn't able to see a contract so I can't help more than that, but I will say what I always say, READ IT!

Remember, Worker's Compensation is for full time employees. After a three month trial period, full insurance benefits including a dental plan are only for casts 1–3, which may take as long as a year to achieve.

During the peak season (summer and Christmas) there is a five day work week and you are allowed to perform six shows a day. No one for any reason may perform more than six shows in one day. Every show is 10–20 minutes of nonstop high energy dancing, singing and stunts. Some are heavily costumed or have heavy make up and all of the shows have pyro special effects.

PYRO

You should remember that every show at Universal has pyro–effects. Flash pot explosives and fire walls all in close proximity to performers. These effects are wonderful for the audiences, especially at night, but for the dancers it's an extra hazard. Stunt performers have worked with pyro from the very beginning of their careers, but dancers have not. If I were performing in one of these shows, I would pay very close attention during rehearsals as to where and when these pyro–effects are going to happen.

MONEY

Once hired you will enter into a rehearsal period of 2–6 weeks depending on the show. ASK! Your rehearsal pay is on a hourly wage, somewhere between $9 and $12 per hour, depending on the show. You will also make an hourly wage when you eventually train other casts. You see, casts 1–3 will train and clean up performances of casts 4–6.

Show pay is another story. You are paid per show up to six shows per day and the show pay varies greatly. In "An American Tail" a dancer will make $16 per show and in "Miami Vice" a performer will make over $50 per show. Remember a show is 10–20 minutes long.

Lets use a show in the middle as our example. Show pay for "Beetlejuice" is $35 per show. During the peak summer season "Beetlejuice" may be performed up to 15 times in one day, as an example let's say you're in cast 3 and you perform 5 shows from 3 P.M. to 8 P.M. That's $175 a day for 5 hours work.   Multiply that for a five day work week and an ambitious dancer can make a very nice salary. Including full medical and dental benefits, stable long term employment and the ability to perform industry jobs outside of the theme park and you have a place of employment few dance jobs can match.

As a dance job, Universal Studios and Las Vegas have similarities.   Both are excellent for young dancers to gain experience, make contacts, and move up the ladder.   They're also a great place for experienced dancers to make a good living, stay in one place and still pursue jobs in films and TV. I am very impressed with Universal Studios Theme Park! I think every dancer should consider it seriously as a great paying dance job, a fun place to work, and an excellent credit on your resumé.

THE AUDITION

As you might expect with seven shows performing and six to seven casts per show, Don Burgess, his assistants and his choreographer are auditioning constantly. They may hold 5 to 10 major auditions a year. The auditions will be advertised in all the trade papers, Drama–Logue, Variety and the Hollywood Reporter. These auditions will draw an enormous amount of dancers. Usually when I ask an Entertainment Director what they look for in a dancer they talk about appearance or dancer ability, but Don Burgess stresses, attitude, attitude, attitude! Universal has a fun, family image. Dancers work very close to the public in many shows, singing and dancing through the crowd, so a good attitude is an important ingredient.

At a major Universal Studios audition, Don Burgess will place a professional stage manager outside the door to pass out application cards to the dancers waiting in line. If you give this manager a hard time or if he observes you arguing or complaining with other dancers, your card will be secretly marked and you'll have a better chance of being held hostage in Iran than getting this job.

One more thing, the shows at Universal Studios Theme park are very specific. "An American Tail" is a show targeting younger children. "Conan" will appeal to all ages, and teenagers will love "Beetlejuice". When Universal auditions for a specific show, they will be explicit in telling you what type of show it is and what type of dancer they are looking for. Pay attention to the audition notice.

Again let's use "Beetlejuice" as an example. "Beetlejuice" is a rock and roll revue. The dance is some jazz, but mostly street and hip hop. The dancers play characters such as Frankenstein, Bride of Frankenstein, Werewolf, and the Phantom of the Opera. The show is fast paced with plenty of rock and roll music and pyro special effects. Dress and look appropriately! I'm not saying come to the audition in full Frankenstein makeup, but don't come wearing ballet slippers and white tights and don't sing something from "Oklahoma". The show is very specific and they know exactly what they're looking for.

Six Flags Over America

Our third example under the heading of theme parks will be "Six Flags Over America". Six Flags currently has 10 parks in the U.S. Cities such as Atlanta, Dallas and Los Angeles are all home to a huge Six Flags theme park.

The example show I want to use is a production of "Teenage Mutant Ninja Turtles." Similar to the movie, Teenage Mutant Ninja Turtles dance, sing and battle the forces of evil on–stage. The Teenage Mutant Ninja Turtles show has been created to perform one week at each Six Flags park in America. For the dancers, this is not just a job at a theme park, but also a mini tour.

Tom White and Patti Columbo have been hired to direct and choreograph this particular production. Tom White's production company has been subcontracted by Six Flags to package this show. Packaging a show can mean conceiving, creating, costuming, casting and rehearsing. What this means to the dancer is, although you will be performing at Six Flags, you will not necessarily be an employee of Six Flags. You will be responsible to and paid by the production company.

Remember production companies vary greatly. Some will pay well. Some don't. Some will have insurance benefits. Some won't. Some will have concern for dancers needs. Some won't.

So let's look at an example of a quality production company and a terrific non–union job for young dancers.

Patti Columbo is a dancer I've worked with on many projects. She has developed into a high energy choreographer who's very much in demand. She's also done an equity version of Teenage Mutant Ninja Turtles that is now touring. I caught up with her in rehearsals of the Six Flags mini–tour Teenage Mutant Ninja Turtles.

DM: *Teenage Mutant Ninja Turtles! They are really hot right now. How was the turnout for this job and where did you audition?*

PC: We held auditions in San Francisco and Los Angeles. I would say we had around 100 people at each call.

DM: *Wow! That's over 200 dancers. How many did you hire?*

PC: Seven. Five leads and two understudies.

DM: *What are some unique problems with this type of show?*

PC: With the original equity show we needed singer/dancer/actors because they used their own voices, but with this show because of logistics and costuming all the singing and speaking will be on soundtrack. That was initially disappointing to some dancers. They will now be lip–synching while doing the choreography. The main problem to overcome is costuming. When you're playing a Ninja turtle you're in costume from head to foot. It's heavy, it's hot and it can make you feel claustrophobic. It's a little harder to hear, a little harder to see. It takes some getting used to.

DM: *How did that affect casting?*

PC: Well, you need strong dancers. The average age of the cast hired is 19. You also have to have dancers with a good attitude. Of course that's important at any call.

DM: *OK. Speaking of any call. Tell me about Patti Columbo's audition.*

PC: Well, the first thing I notice is appearance. I would remind dancers that what you wear is immediately important. It says a lot about you. You won't see me doing a long dance combination. I think long dance calls are stupid. I can tell a good dancer within two counts of eight. The other things I look for are high energy and a good attitude. You can always tell a dancer with a good attitude right away. A dancer should be aware they are auditioning the entire time they're in the dance studio. I make it a point to watch dancers on the side of the room when they're not dancing. I want to see how they relate to other dancers. Are they friendly? Are they keeping their energy focused. Things like that.

DM: *Do you ever type dancers out right away?*

PC: No! Very rarely and certainly not for this show since you're in costume and looks mean absolutely nothing. I like to make my first cut on dancer ability.

DM: *Name a pet peeve. Something that really bothers you at an audition.*

PC: Oh! When a dancer asks all kinds of questions just to get noticed. If you have a question about a dance step... of course ask it. But don't keep asking questions just to get attention. That really bothers me. Also, I really can't take the "I'm too cool for this" attitude. That will get you cut from my audition right away. I remember sitting in my kitchen after a final callback. I was with my assistant choreographer and we were looking at the pictures of 15 terrific dancers. Unfortunately, we could only hire six. I held up a picture of a dancer I didn't know very well. I asked my assistant, "Is she fun to work with?" He shook his head, "I worked with her before, she's very difficult to work with." GONE! Seriously, there's too much to do in a short time to work with someone who's not going to try to make it enjoyable.

DM: *Other choreographers have said, picking up the combination quickly at the audition isn't important. Is that the case with you?*

PC: I wish I could say yes, but I can't. Money is tight with most shows today and there isn't always enough time to rehearse. Teenage Mutant Ninja Turtles is a one hour show of dance number after dance number. There's an awful lot to learn and picking up the combination quickly at the audition lets me know you're a fast learner.

DM: *I've worked with you and I've auditioned for you. At the audition I've always felt you're really behind the dancer.*

PC: Always! I know how hard it is. I know how badly people want the job. How serious they are. I try to encourage them at the call but I also feel if a dancer's prepared they will work a lot.

DM: *By prepared you mean good training?*

PC: Yes! Good training. This show is a little different than most. It's primarily high energy street dancing, but when I was auditioning for "On The Town", I needed dancers who could do all types of dance. Ballet, jazz, partner work, plus be able to sing and handle some acting. There are very few dancers like that. Even in a city as large as Los Angeles, there are very few. A well rounded, well trained dancer is invaluable!

I want to thank Patti Columbo for her insight in helping the young dancer. I'd like to quickly go through the work and money aspects of Teenage Mutant Ninja Turtles giving you a better idea of whether or not you want to pursue this type of work.

WORK

This is a ten week tour. You will be spending 1 week (six working days per week) at a different Six Flags theme park. You will perform 2 shows per day, which I have to say is minimal. Most theme park productions perform five or six times a day. The show is fast paced, heavily costumed and runs about an hour. I remember Patti saying "prepare to lose weight and drink plenty of fluid.". The rehearsal period is two weeks long, six days a week, 10:00 AM – 6:00 PM with a break for lunch. The dancers will be flying commercially between cities – a big plus if you've ever done a bus and truck tour. Tom White (the Director/Producer) makes sure that every dancer has a contract and a complete agenda of the tour at the beginning of rehearsals. Again, I want to say this is a professional and caring production company. They are not all the same.

Ask for a contract. Ask for an agenda of the tour. Ask if there is per diem. Ask if there is worker's compensation if you're hurt on the stage. And ask these questions on the first day of rehearsal, not halfway into the tour.

MONEY

The pay for this mini–tour is $600 per week. Compare that to other non–union dance jobs and you'll probably show up at the next audition. There is also a $30 per diem to help with expenses on the tour. Of course, airline travel is paid for and you'll be staying at first rate hotels in or near the park. Another important thing to know is there will be a

Company Manager on the tour with you. A Company Manager takes care of many problems but one of the most important things they do is to make sure you get paid each week. They will also make arrangements with a local bank in each city to get your check cashed and take care of other banking needs.

PER DIEM

Per diem, in this case $30 per day, is usually given to the dancer in cash. Sometimes at the start of the week, sometimes at the end of the week with your check. Remember per diem is not just free cash. You will have to declare it as income at tax time. In order to offset per diem income you need to keep receipts of your expenses on the road and keep good tax records.

CHAPTER FIVE

CRUISE LINES

All cruise lines are not the same. They cater to different groups of people, they vary in length, expense and entertainment. For the dancer, this means different pay, different work expectations and various living arrangements. It's not my intention to tell you about every cruise line and rate them as an employer. It is my intention to use a certain cruise line as an example of what to expect and more importantly, what questions to ask.

Kloster Cruise Limited owns Royal Viking Lines, Royal Cruise Lines, and Norwegian Cruise Lines. Even within Kloster, jobs for the dancer vary. Let's start at the top. Royal Viking Lines (RVL) is one of the best, if not the best cruise line on the water today. The cruises are mostly two weeks in length but they also have world cruises 100 days in length. Royal Viking is a first class cruise line for passengers and employees. I want you to evaluate whatever cruise line you may be considering against what RVL has to offer. Let's start with the personnel of RVL.

Morag Veljkovic is the Entertainment Manager for Royal Viking. She's not just a business person who sits behind a desk. She's been a dancer, teacher and choreographer for many years. This is very important since the choreographer is once again your lifeline to the job ahead. This is the person you need to ask all the right questions <u>before</u> you take the job. Another benefit to having Morag as Entertainment Manager, is that she's compassionate to the needs of a dancer, having been there many times herself.

About the choreographer, I know it's impossible for every dancer to know every choreographer but if you have some background on the choreographer you're auditioning for, it is helpful. Tommy Tune loves personalities, of course, with great tap training. Michael Peters loves trained dancers with street rhythm and an individual style. So if Morag will let me, I'm going to give you some background about her with a few of her quotes.

Training:

"Don't come near me without solid training."

"Dance fads, like Hip Hop, come and go but a dancer trained in ballet, jazz, and tap will always work."

"A dancer who can sing is valuable in today's market."

Appearance:

"The audiences on Royal Viking Lines are older, wealthy, and fairly conservative. I need a well groomed, well behaved, well dressed dancer. If I

have that, I can get the dancer more benefits on the ship. They are an asset to the cruise line."

"If you come to my audition unkempt I'm going to assume that's how you would be on the ship."

"If you come to the audition wearing loose baggy clothes, I'm going to assume you're plump."

Attitude:

"I need a dancer who wants to work. A one hundred day cruise is no place to get lazy."

"If I see a dancer with a good attitude, tries hard and takes direction, I know I can work with them."

Compassion:

"At the audition I am pulling for you, it makes my job easier. A dancer should know, I want you to be good."

"Every dancer kept to the end will receive a phone call or a letter. As a dancer I always hated not knowing what happened. You will be kept on file and considered in the future."

Before you move on, I'd like to stress one more point about Morag Veljkovic. Not only is she a quality choreographer, but more importantly for the young dancer, she's a great teacher. A conscientious dancer taking a six month contract on Royal Viking Lines couldn't help coming out a better performer.

WORK

Most of the cruises on Royal Viking Lines are two weeks in length but there are one hundred day world cruises. On the two week cruise you will perform four or five different shows. These are fast–paced highly costumed shows of song and dance. Morag gave me some examples; "History of Dance Revue", narrated by Cydd Charisse, "A Tribute to Cole Porter", "A Tribute to Broadway."

These shows have book, lyrics and choreography, so there's a lot to learn.

On the one hundred day world cruise, dancers become a repertory company. Really! As you can imagine, keeping the same passengers entertained on a three and a half month cruise is a lot of work. You will be performing one show at night and rehearsing another show during the day to be performed two or three days later.

REHEARSAL

You've landed the job! You've signed a six month contract and now you're flying to Miami to rehearse.

You can expect to rehearse four to six weeks, six days a week from 10:00 a.m. to 6:00 p.m. Rehearsal periods are always difficult but you'll be glad you're working for someone who knows dancers. There are ample breaks and an hour for lunch. You'll be working for half salary plus per diem during this rehearsal period. Per diem varies so – ASK! Transportation and hotel is covered, but don't expect to run up your room service bill and get away with it. All phone calls and expenses in the hotel are to be paid by you.

ALMOST READY TO SAIL

Before you sail you'll need a physical. This is paid for by Royal Viking Lines and upon passing your physical, your medical insurance begins.

You'll need a passport! All dancers should have passports, so I won't get into that again.

You'll also need to fill out a work visa which again Royal Viking Lines will pay for.

Morag suggests making copies of visas and passports, especially since passports will be held on the ship. Don't panic! The reason they are held is not to hold you hostage. Your passports are held because the ship passes through so many different countries and passports must be checked and stamped in each country. When you turn in your passport you will receive your crew card ID. This card will act as your passport and identification while you're an employee. You'll need your crew card to get on and off the ship.

GOING TO SEA

Every dancer hired will be sent a complete package, and I mean complete.

1. You'll receive a six month contract. As always, read it! I will cover some particulars of the contract but not all!

2. You will receive an itinerary. Not only a flight date to Miami for rehearsal, but how long you'll rehearse and when you'll report to your ship. The second half of this itinerary will tell you which ship you'll be on and where it will travel.

3. You'll receive a manual telling you everything you need to know about your job on the Royal Viking Lines. What to bring? What benefits you have? This manual is updated constantly. It's one of the most informative guides I've ever seen in any dance job.

4. You'll receive complete books of scripted shows and audio cassettes with vocals and without vocals so you can practice at home. Dancers who sing are expected to know lyrics before rehearsal.

Morag and staff have worked very hard to make this package complete. When you have all your questions answered before leaving for rehearsal it can really reduce your stress level.

WORK DUTY

In your contract with Royal Viking Lines you'll notice that you are obligated to perform a work duty besides your show performance. Read it carefully! These duty obligations are different from ship to ship. Some cruise lines don't schedule work duty for dancers. Others don't have work duty for principals, just chorus. Here are a few things you should know about work duty:

1. The Cruise Director is ultimately in charge of work duty although the line captain from the cast may designate specific jobs.

2. Work duty is usually a sport, game or event. You will help coordinate the event; i.e. Ping Pong Tournament or Water Volleyball.

3. Your one work duty per day will be no longer than two hours and not later than noon on show days. This is in your contract! Some Cruise Directors will try to take advantage of the situation and get you to work longer. Remember, you don't have to if you don't want to. This brings me to my next point.

4. I've had friends who've gotten restless on a cruise ship after 3 or 4 months and wanted to work other duty events. If you want to work more than one duty event, you can, but don't let your performance suffer.

MONEY

Once again, we'll see that monetary benefits don't always mean cold hard cash, but let's start with money. A dancer will earn between $325 – $650 dollars per week depending on three things:

1. The amount of time you've worked for Royal Viking Lines. They do compensate dancers who want to stay on for more than one contract.

2. The cruise line you're working on. Remember Kloster Cruise Limited owns Royal Viking Lines, Royal Cruise Lines, and Norwegian Cruise Lines and the salary may vary according to the cruise lines and the length of the cruise.

3. The third consideration is ability. A dancer who can swing parts, understudy principal parts or work as a line captain can earn extra cash.

Remember, your rehearsal pay will be one half of salary negotiated.

LIVING QUARTERS

Nothing can affect your experience working on a cruise ship quite like your living arrangements. If I were going back out on a ship, this would be the first question I would ask! When I worked on Norwegian Cruise Lines in 1988, principals had their own passenger cabin. Chorus dancers had to share crew cabins with another dancer.

The difference is unbelievable!

The passenger cabins are very nice. They're carpeted, have TV's, phones, and plenty of room for one person. OK, now don't laugh, but you should ask to have an outside cabin with a porthole. I didn't even consider a porthole a benefit until I was out to sea for awhile. You learn to love that window, especially when you spend thirty minutes in a cabin without a porthole.

Crew cabins are smaller, and shared by two people. They usually have bunk beds, linoleum on the floor (instead of carpet) and few with portholes. ASK!

The biggest downside of a crew cabin, to me, is the fact that other members of the crew are on the same level and work different shifts. The crew cabins are always on the lower levels, so with bare walls and linoleum on the floor, the noise level is enhanced. It's not bad if you're in the party mood but if you're trying to get some sleep it can take a major adjustment.

On Royal Viking Lines every dancer has their own cabin! Again, this is not just to praise Royal Viking Lines, it's for you to know what's available on some cruise lines and to use Royal Viking Lines as an example.

BANKING

A cruise ship has almost a full service bank on board and you will have your own account. I say almost, because I don't think they have everything. Your checks can be directly deposited into your account and you can draw on that money anytime. Take full advantage of using your account to save money. It's difficult to find your next dance job from the ship, so the money you save will help a lot when you head back home.

Many dancers have saved a lot of money, returned home for a year or two and decided to do another six month contract.

Probably the greatest benefit to working on Royal Viking Lines is the number of countries you'll visit. You can withdraw some of your money in U.S. dollars, see the ships purser on your way ashore and exchange your dollars for the local currency. When you return from your sightseeing you can change it back to U.S. dollars.

OTHER BENEFITS

After signing your second six month contract, you are allowed to bring two friends or relatives on the cruise with you for 25% of regular fare.

Royal Viking Lines will pay for one hundred pounds of excess baggage per six month contract. So if you buy a big stereo in Japan, it won't cost you extra to get it home.

You'll also have a return plane ticket in your name when you arrive in Miami. No fear of being stranded anywhere.

LIFESTYLE

Is there a better way to make a living? You're visiting countries you may never get to see again, eating fine food, traveling on a world class ship, dancing and being paid for it. This is a terrific job for dancers young and old yet many dancers don't realize it. I was able to watch the audition process in Los Angeles for Royal Viking. Morag was in the middle of a nationwide tour auditioning dancers and singer-dancers. Cities like New York, Los Angeles, Chicago, Houston, Miami, Orlando, and San Francisco are all stops on this tour. I couldn't believe the turnout! Maybe twenty-five dancer-singers showed up, and out of twenty-five, Morag could hire three. I know how many dancers are unemployed in Los Angeles, and I couldn't believe there weren't 100 dancers there. I know some dancers don't want to leave town, but I have to believe many dancers don't know what a great job this is! I've also heard dancers around the country complain how few dance jobs come to their town and yet Morag told me 6 or 7 dancers showed up for the audition in Houston.

I want dancers to know which non-union dance jobs are worthwhile. RVL is one of them. You'll earn decent money, be able to save money, (not having to pay for food and lodging) and you'll be getting stage time which can only make you a better dancer. This is a great job for the young and for the experienced dancer.

OK! We've talked about living arrangements, now let's talk about my favorite... FOOD! This is the second question I would ask before taking a job at sea. On some cruise lines dancers eat with the rest of the crew in the crew mess. If it sounds like the military, it is, only the food's not as good. Then there are the cruise lines that have a separate mess for entertainers. The food is usually a little better but just a step above crew mess. It's like eating in a cafeteria for six months. Then there is RVL, where you will be seated at a table in the passenger dining room and will be served anything on the passenger menu.

Morag has fought hard for this benefit. She had to explain to Kloster the benefit of having you with the passengers. As you know, the public loves entertainers and is always curious as to what your life is like. In essence, you will be hosting the table. You will be a representative of Royal Viking at the table. A small price to pay for being served fine food and wine. Speaking of wine, Morag and RVL have thought of everything. If a passenger buys a bottle of wine for the table, you can reciprocate and buy a bottle tomorrow night without having to spend your own money. You get a monthly wine and bar allowance! Do you believe that! Eating in the passenger dining room as opposed to the crew mess and a wine and bar allowance! These are reasons RVL is to be compared to other cruise lines

Hold on! There is a downside to great food. Weigh–ins! If you decide to overindulge or not exercise enough, you could find yourself back home early. If weight is a problem you should consider this now. Weigh–ins will be held every two weeks and if your weight changes drastically from your weight at your physical you will be warned. If it doesn't correct itself, you may be terminated.

CLOTHES

With other dance jobs you perform your shows and go home. On RVL, anytime you're on the passenger decks, you're representing RVL, even when you're not performing, hostessing, or performing a work duty. If you're having a drink out on pool deck or in one of the piano bars there still exists a certain protocol. Morag is able to get the dancers certain benefits by convincing RVL that your visibility is an asset to the line. This means your behavior and your clothing must follow certain guidelines. Start with common sense.

If you're headed to the pool deck from your cabin, a bathing suit may be appropriate for the pool but not for other areas you may pass through. Cover up!

The main clothing concern for dancers working the ship is formal wear. For men, this means a tuxedo. For women, this means a gown or cocktail dress. Some cruise ships have formal nights; i.e. Tuesday and Thursday nights you must have formal wear. On other lines you must have formal wear on passenger decks every evening after 6 PM.

Men: If you don't have a tuxedo, you'll need to buy one. If you can afford to buy more than one, do it. If you can't afford more than one, buy as many different accessories as you can. Different colored bow ties and cummerbunds can dress up the tuxedo.

Women: Of course it's more difficult for women. It's impossible to change a gown like a man can change a tuxedo. Bring as many formal dresses as you can. Buy them, if you can, borrow them if you have to, but bring them. You'll need them.

DRILL PRECAUTIONS

You may be cruising on a thousand foot vessel, ten stories high, weighing hundreds of tons, but when you're in a storm in the middle of the ocean, you won't believe how insignificant you feel. Take drill seriously.

At least once a cruise you will practice a lifeboat drill. Every passenger and staff member has a seat on a lifeboat. Your lifeboat number and directions to it are on the backside of your cabin door. As a staff member you may have another duty before heading to your lifeboat. It may be assisting passengers with their life jackets. You will be well trained on drill and your duties. Pay attention, it could be very important. Occasionally, the Coast Guard will hold a drill onboard and evaluate the ship.

CLASS

Not being able to audition for other jobs while you're working and not being able to take class are negatives to cruising, but you can adjust.

Although you won't be able to study with other choreographers, you can stay in great shape onboard. There is always a core of dedicated dancers who want to excel at their craft.   When I worked the ships there was a well trained dancer, superior to the rest of us, who would give us a good workout and combination two or three times a week. It was great! We would make it more fun by each creating a few counts of eight of the dance combination. I would take the first two counts of eight then the next person would pick it up and add their own two counts of eight.   There is also a full warm up, physically and vocally before every performance. Bottom line, if you want to stay in shape, you can do it on the ship, but meeting new choreographers and learning their styles will have to wait till you get home.

DRUGS

For those of you that don't do drugs you can skip this section, but if you do, you better think again before you bring them on the ship. If you are caught with drugs, the least that will happen is you'll be sent home, but there is always the chance you'll have charges brought against you.

Three things to think about:

1. There are crew members who are informants.

2. The ship I went on had periodic drug searches where drug sniffing dogs were brought through the cabins.

3. On the Islands in the Caribbean a few passengers and crew were foolish enough to

purchase marijuana. They would get about a block away and be arrested. It's a big scam on the Islands where someone sells you pot and his brother the cop arrests you. The cop scares the hell out of you, makes you pay a large fine and lets you go. He gives the pot back to his brother and they do it again to the next fool!

TID BITS

The Shore Excursion Director is in charge of shore tours in all ports of call. These tours may consist of horseback riding, boat rides, hiking to a waterfall, or seeing the pyramids. The passengers will usually pay extra for shore excursions. Get to know the shore excursion director! Many times if there is room available you can go on the tour for free. While I'm on the subject, it's important to treat not just the cast but fellow crew members with courtesy and respect. The crew notices that you are a crew member with special benefits and sometimes they resent that. If you're friendly and appreciative to your fellow crew members, you'll find they can make your life much easier. Once, the cast did a special show late at night for crew members not on duty. Not only was it well received, but for weeks, complimentary drinks would come my way or a cook would place an extra lobster tail on my plate. What goes around, comes around.

STAGE

Dancers always have to adjust to different stages but how often do you work on a moving stage? Forgot about that, Huh? This is something you may never get used to. Some nights the water is calm and the dancing is easy, but some nights it's difficult to keep your balance standing still. Try a pirouette! Leaps and jumps are difficult for two reasons:

1. When you leap into the air the stage is not in the same place when you land. Sometimes it's closer—sometimes it's farther away.

2. The other problem I had with leaps is the low ceiling. Remember this is a cruise ship first, an entertainment center second. I would jump into the air and hit my hands on the lights. Also, be careful if you're involved in lifts.

QUESTIONS TO ASK

Whatever cruise line you're considering, the answers to the following questions are a must:

1. Salary

2. Rehearsal Pay and Per Diem

3. Work Duty

4. Living Arrangements

5. Eating Arrangements

CRUISE LINES AND CRUISE SHIP COMPANIES

You can submit pictures and resumés to these cruise lines.

Royal Viking

Attn: Morag Veljkovic
95 Merrick Way
Coral Gables, FL 33134
(305) 460-4793

Royal Caribbean

Attn: Robin Cahill
1050 Caribbean Way
Miami, FL 33132
(305) 379-2601

Princess Cruises

10100 Santa Monica Blvd.
Los Angeles, CA 90067
(310) 553-1770

Carnival Cruise Lines

3655 N.W. 87th Avenue
Miami, FL 33178
(305) 599-2500

Sitmar Cruises

10100 Santa Monica Blvd.
Los Angeles, CA 90067
(310) 553-1666

Crystal Cruises

2121 Avenue of the Stars
Los Angeles, CA 90067
(310) 785-9300

Cunard Lines

555 Fifth Avenue
New York, NY 10017
(212) 880-7500

Jean Ann Ryan Prod's

Cunard & Royal Norwegian
308 S.E. 14th Street
Ft. Lauderdale, FL 33316
(305) 523-6414

CHAPTER SIX

LAS VEGAS

Intro: Interview with Larry Lee; Entertainment Director of the Tropicana Hotel.

Discussion topic: "Folies Bergere".

DM: *Larry, how many people in the cast?*

LL: There are 54 people in the "Folies".

DM: *And there are three different lines of dancers?*

LL: Right. Acrobatic dancers, dressed dancers and nude dancers, (meaning topless in some numbers) and of course showgirls.

DM: *Let's talk specifically about dancers. Is there a height requirement?*

LL: Actually, no. We try to match the girls at an audition, and match the girls to the ones we have left, but we have made allowances with a girl auditioning who might be a few inches taller or shorter. We do try to keep some type of uniformity if we can. I would say 5'6" to 5'8" is about right for women, 5'10" to 6'2" for men.

DM: *What about acro–dancers?*

LL: Well, some acro–dancers are traditionally shorter, and we're mainly concerned with good acrobatic ability.

DM: *How many dancers in each line?*

LL: In each line, there are six girls and six boy dancers. There are also six extras who rotate positions allowing for emergencies and extra days off.

DM: *How often do you hold auditions?*

LL: What we like to do is this. Whether we have an opening or not, we will still give a dancer an audition. We will call back those people we like and re–audition them when we do have an opening.

DM: *So in essence, anyone submitting for an audition will get one?*

LL: Yes. Our Company Manager, Laura Garbett, will file their picture and resumé and call those people first, when we do have an opening.

DM: *A little insight into an audition. What is expected of a dancer at the audition?*

LL: Well, first off, dancing ability, both jazz and ballet, but mostly jazz for our present show. We're looking for style, technique, and then of course overall appearance and stage presence.

DM: *So dancewear for the audition should be geared toward jazz?*

LL: Yes, jazzwear for men, and women definitely in heels, leotards and tights. No flats or ballet slippers.

DM: *Tell me a story about mistakes dancers make at auditions*

LL: Laura Garbett and I feel the same way on this. We try to make the audition as painless as possible. We know what dancers go through with training and auditioning, and we try to make them feel comfortable. I hate the "cattle call". I think its demeaning. So I try not to embarrass anyone no matter how limited they are, but it never fails, there is always someone who thinks they can get up on stage and do the choreography we do in the show just because they dance well in a disco or something. You must have training.

DM: *Larry, you know how hard the show is, how much training would you estimate a dancer needs?*

LL: Different people excel faster than others, but I would say a minimum of five years training is needed to do what we do.

DM: *What's the work schedule like?*

LL: Two shows a night, six nights a week, and it's rather demanding to do a schedule like that. The show is dark on Thursdays and we close for two weeks in December.

DM: *What about the contract?*

LL: Dancers hired will sign a six month contract. At the Tropicana Hotel they have a fantastic health and insurance policy. They're a Tropicana employee and have the same dental and medical benefits.

DM: *After a six month contract do all dancers have to re–audition?*

LL: We don't have re–auditions, but they will be evaluated during that first six month period and asked to sign again.

DM: *So one of the great things about dancing in Vegas is the possibility of long term work.*

LL: Absolutely!

MONEY

In discussing the wages and benefits for the working dancer in a Las Vegas revue, I have to separate the work into two categories: Production shows and Lounge shows. Here are a few examples of each:

Production shows:

Tropicana's "Folies Bergere"

Splash

Jubilee

City Lights

Enter the Night

Lounge shows:

Bare Essence

Legends in Concert

Naughty Girls

Brazilia

PRODUCTION SHOWS

Production shows consist of large casts, as noted in the interview, and equally large budgets (upwards of 5 million dollars). The stage area is huge, and can easily swallow up the average Broadway stage. The showrooms are capable of seating 1500–2000 people per show and will be filled to capacity on many evenings. Working a production show can be very exciting. Now, lets get to the important topic—MONEY.

Simply, the cast will be separated into two large groups, Principals and chorus dancers.

PRINCIPALS

Principals will consist of lead singers, including a master of ceremonies if there is one, lead adagio dancers, and principal dancers. These performers will receive a principal contract, special billing, and perform some type of featured number. As you might have guessed a "Principal" is in more of a position to negotiate money than a chorus dancer and their salaries show just that. Principal salaries vary from $650 to $1500 a week as of late 1992. One of the great things about a Vegas show is the possibility of a hard working chorus dancer moving up into a principal position and reaping the financial rewards that come with it. Remember, female principal dancers and lead adagio dancers are almost always topless.

CHORUS DANCERS

A chorus dancer is any dancer dancing in a group or "line" of dancers.

For the men, there is usually one line consisting of anywhere from 6 to 20 dancers. For the women, the chorus lines are separated into "covered" and "nude" or "topless" dancers.

The "Folies Bergere" is an exception, adding lines of both male and female "Acro–dancers". The male dancer and "covered" dancer will receive the same $485 to $525 a week, depending on the show.

The "nude" dancers will receive anywhere from $50 to $75 more per week and will usually be more featured in the show.

Most production shows pay half salaries for the initial rehearsal period, usually a two week period while you're learning the show. They also pay $150 per week for rehearsing new numbers while performing the old show at night.

BENEFITS

Although Nevada is a "Right to Work" state it really doesn't apply since there isn't a union covering dancers at this time. AGVA, a union for "variety artists" made an attempt to unionize in the late 1970's, but for some reason never received any real support.

Dancers in production shows are employees of the company that owns the hotel in which the show is performed. Let me show you an example: The "Folies Bergere" performed in the Tropicana Hotel is owned by Aztar Inc. and all performers are Aztar employees, receiving the same benefits as other Aztar employees.

HAS THAT SUNK IN YET?

Very seldom, if ever, do non–union dancers receive full medical, dental, worker's compensation, and unemployment insurance. You also have the possibility of Credit Unions, buying company stock and establishing seniority as an employee. Almost makes you feel like a real person — doesn't it?!

All joking aside, this is one of the greatest things about working in a Vegas production show. When you combine wages, benefits and the cost of living in Nevada, working in a production might be an option for you.

THE LOUNGE SHOW

The lounge show has been very successful in Nevada for many years. Unlike the production show, taking place in large showrooms, these smaller reviews perform in lounges (a room seating anywhere from 150–450 people per show). The stage area is much smaller and production values are not on as grand a scale, but don't misunderstand, the lounge show, with a cast of 10–25 dancers and a little creativity, can be a powerhouse of entertainment.

According to many dancers who prefer lounge shows, the feeling is the smaller cast enables them to be seen as an individual performer. Remember, production shows have casts of 50 and up. It could be said every dancer in a lounge show is a featured dancer and has a great opportunity to showcase their talent.

Another strong point for the lounge show is because of a smaller budget and shortage of space for sets, the choreography and dance values become the focal point in the review. You will find the pace of the lounge show very fast. The dance sequences with fast costume changes move along in rapid fire succession. Dancers in lounge shows typically enjoy the choreography, which is usually much more challenging. Although this type of work is very exciting, it's also very demanding. The lounge show can perform three one–hour shows nightly, or up to eighteen shows a week.

In a production show, you'll be an employee of the hotel in which you work. In a lounge show, you may be hired, work for and get paid by a production company producing this particular show. THIS IS IMPORTANT! Production companies vary greatly in contracts, pay, benefits and conditions. Let's look into it.

After you're hired, you'll receive a contract. READ IT! I know they're dull and difficult to understand, but take the time to read it and know it. I'll show you examples of both production show and lounge show contracts on the following pages. Don't expect to receive all the information you need to know from the producer. There is nothing worse than working for a few weeks and finding 'surprises' in your paycheck, only to be told to _read your contract_.

Let me give you three examples of payment and tax structures you might find working for different production companies in lounge shows:

Example 1

What used to be the rule is a show like "Legends In Concert." The show has four to eight chorus people. They pay $100–$150 per week for rehearsal and $400–$500 a week for performances. A week consists of two shows a night for six nights. Your Federal withholding, FICA, Social Security, and Unemployment Insurance taxes are taken out of your paycheck automatically. You pay a percentage of your S.S. and U.I. tax and the employer pays a percentage. You'll receive Worker's Compensation if injured on the job, but like most lounge shows, they have no medical or dental programs.

Example 2

A lounge show similar to "DanSin Dirdy". Again, you'll receive $100–$150 per week for rehearsal, and that period could be as long as eight weeks before opening the show. Dancers receive $450–$500 a week performing two or sometimes three shows a night for six nights. The big difference in Example 2 is you'll be hired as an independent contractor. This means as far as taxes go, you'll be responsible for setting aside your own Federal, FICA, and SS taxes—they won't be deducted automatically. This will call for a very disciplined person to put aside the money due your tax account each quarter. If you don't put aside a certain amount of money for taxes, you could find yourself owing the IRS a large sum of money at the end of the year, including penalties for not filing quarterly estimated taxes. To avoid these problems, you may want to contact an accountant regarding the responsibilities of an independent contractor. Many dancers have gotten into trouble with this type of producer contract, but if you're a disciplined working dancer and keep good tax records then you can make this work for you.

Example 3

Other producers have lounge show contracts like "Hallelujah–Las Vegas," which independently contracts dancers, but instead of paying a regular salary, pays a percentage of gross ticket sales. Now before you start seeing dollar signs all over, stop, and think for a moment. Again, you will have to pay your own taxes, *and* your pay will fluctuate based on how well the show has done in a given week. I've never been in a show like this personally, but I've heard the "sweet" and "sour" sides to this type of show. I've talked with dancers bragging about their $687 week, only to find them grumbling about their $237 a week later. When the rent is due and the audiences are thin, the grumbling can be severe. There is another problem with this type of payment. Although there are honest producers out there, I don't know how a dancer can perform <u>and</u> keep track of the amount of money coming into a lounge room.

Like I said, with every producer there are different types of contracts and payments. These are just three examples of the multitude of combinations to be aware of. Lounge shows can be very exciting, challenging and fun, but only if you know your contract, your responsibilities and how you will be paid. Little "surprises" along the way, like tax problems or a lower than expected salary can take the fun out.

WORK

There's no doubt about it, talking about money is fun, but let me share with you what's expected for the dollars you receive. It's called work, and I want you to understand ahead of time how much of it you'll be obligated to perform for the money and benefits described in the previous section. I'm going to cover the highlights of a typical production contract. Although they do vary slightly, I think this is a good example of the quality and quantity of work expected of a dancer in a production show.

This sample agreement between the Tropicana Hotel and Dancer is current as of the 21st of January, 1992. There may be slight changes in the future, but remember this is only an example. The contract we'll be looking into is actually seven pages long.

1. DUTIES AND TERM OF EMPLOYMENT

Employee hereby accepts employment with employer under the direction, supervision, and control of Employer and the Employer's Director of Entertainment for the period commencing...

This section will state the type of dancer position hired for and the length of time that your contract is valid. Most production show contracts are six months but may be up to one year in length. An example in assumption of this section might read; "Employer hereby accepts employment as a Regular Covered

Dancer commencing February 1, 1992 and terminating July 31, 1992."

2. PERFORMANCES

Employee shall be required to perform two or three shows nightly, or up to thirteen shows in a six day week with one day off. Employee is also required to attend up to three hours of "brush–up" rehearsal. Unused brush–up rehearsal hours are accruable over the duration of the show (or contract).

This really means if you don't rehearse this week, next week the producer could rehearse you six hours without additional pay. Since no one keeps track of these "unused brush–up" rehearsal hours, a producer could conceivably call you in at any time for any number of hours rehearsal.

3. PUBLICITY

Employee shall make themselves available for any and all publicity, and is not entitled to any compensation, fees, royalties, or other remuneration.

Simply put, you will perform any publicity the employer deems advantageous to the hotel for your regular salary and nothing more.

4. PERFORMANCE STANDARD

Employee will perform their duties in accordance with the highest standards of quality. The Director of Entertainment will continuously monitor the show and have absolute discretion in insuring that such standards of quality are maintained. Failure to maintain such performance standards is a breach of contract and good cause for termination.

This means the Entertainment Director's opinion is law, as to whether your performance level is equal to that of your fellow dancers. If he feels it's not, you could be fired.

5. PERSONAL APPEARANCE

Employee agrees to maintain the same weight and general appearance that existed at the time employee was hired.

EXAMPLE: If you gain weight you'll be given a weight notice and weighed. You'll then be given a certain amount of time to lose weight or face the possibility of termination. Oh yes, if you're thinking about getting a blue mohawk haircut and putting a ring in your nose after you're hired, THINK AGAIN!

6. REPORTING FOR PERFORMANCES

There is a half–hour call before most shows. You must sign in at least a half–hour before a performance or rehearsal. If you're late you could be assessed a $25 fine. Three late arrivals during the term of this contract may be cause for dismissal.

7. EXCLUSIVITY

Employee hereby agrees that during the term of this Agreement Employee will render

Employee's sole and exclusive services in the entertainment business and media, whether on stage or in moving pictures or on radio or television or otherwise, TO EMPLOYER ONLY, and will not render any such services nor appear publicly for any other person, firm or corporation without first obtaining the written consent of the Director of Entertainment.

The Employers of most production shows are very lenient with this clause. I know of many dancers, including myself who have moonlighted frequently in other types of entertainment (commercials, movies, conventions). This clause is the Employers protection of their show. I have seen Entertainment Directors come down hard on dancers who work another job all day, only to call in sick for the show at night, or their performance at night suffers because of the fatigue from working the extra job. This is an example of how a few dancers have spoiled it for many. Although it's very seldom used, remember this clause is in the contract and you could be terminated for performing in another type of work in the entertainment business without written consent.

8. TERMINATION OF AGREEMENT

This Agreement may be terminated by employer AT ANY TIME, WITHOUT CAUSE, upon two weeks prior written notice to employee.

(Please read section eight in connection with section nine).

9. LIQUIDATED DAMAGES

Employee recognizes and agrees that Employer may incur substantial expenses in employing employee including advertising, auditions, rehearsal pay and fitting and purchase of costumes and accessories, and that the total damages to Employer resulting from a breach or early termination of this Agreement by Employee are difficult to ascertain, and this Employee agrees to pay to Employer the sum of ($1,500) as liquidated damages.

Simply put, under this six month agreement, the dancer may be terminated with or without cause. But, if the dancer decides to quit before the contract is completed, he or she may have to pay the employer $1,500 in "liquidating damages."

It's kind of like going to the bank and being assessed a penalty for early withdrawal for taking out your money. No kidding, this is very important if you're not sure you can commit to the job for the length of the contract. I've known dancers who could have done Broadway shows or other much higher paying jobs, but were faced with the choice of turning them down or coming up with $1,500 in "damages."

These are just some of the highlights in one example of a production show contract. I know hundreds of dancers who have enjoyed working production shows for many years. It is not my intention to steer you away or toward this type of work, but I do want you to know as much as possible about every type of dance job you may become involved in.

Lifestyle

Once again, under the heading of lifestyle there are many advantages and disadvantages to working in Las Vegas. In the hopes of being objective, which is very difficult since I lived there for nine years, let me explain some of the things you will come in contact with and let you ultimately decide if these are positives or negatives.

Vegas is a very exciting 24 hour town, and that does take some getting used to. Restaurants, bars, supermarkets and even some dry cleaners stay open 24 hours. Entertainment is continuous from 1 PM to early into the morning hours. The casinos, of course, never close. I've had my hair cut in a salon at 3 AM, although today, I can't for the life of me remember why. Everything seems to be completely unconcerned with time. I remember my first Saturday night in Vegas. I didn't really know anyone yet, so I decided to hit the most popular nightclub in town, dance a little, and have a few beers. So I cleaned up, tried my best not to look like some guy who just shot up a shopping mall, and headed out. Now I don't know about you but where I come from 10:30 PM is usually a good time to hit a bar. I walked in to a huge, stylish disco with a dance floor you could land a plane on and a light show even the Las Vegas strip would be proud of. I walked over to the bar, sat down, ordered a beer and stared at the other ten people that occupied the entire club. I mean it was empty, I could of yelled "fire" and we all would have had our own exit. Well, about an hour or two beers later (I can be very slow about these things), I asked the bartender if anyone ever frequented this club.   He looked at me kind of strange and said, "Not before midnight."   Sure enough, about ten minutes after twelve the place started to fill up like a rock concert had just let out in the parking lot. The placed smoked from that point on. I started for home about 8 AM, leaving a club packed with people who had no idea that another day had begun without them. I found out later that many nightclubs close whenever the patrons decide to go home. Since then, I've made the necessary adjustments.

Vegas seems to have the best of both worlds. Travel just outside of town and experience the small town feel of a desert community. Slow pace, quiet stillness, desert wildlife are all available, if that's for you. Lake Mead, about 30 minutes away, is the largest man–made lake in the United States. Swimming, fishing, boating, skiing and wind–surfing are activities for people who live in this supposedly barren wasteland. Mt. Charleston, just 50 minutes northwest has beautiful hiking in the summer and a challenging ski resort in the winter.

In town, big name entertainment is everywhere. Sinatra, Cher, Diana Ross, and Ann Margaret are just a few of the headliners. Big time concerts, national rodeo finals, ballooning, off road racing, boxing, ballet, and so many more activities I couldn't possibly name them all. Vegas lifestyle has a lot to offer.

CREDIT

Establishing credit for a dancer can range anywhere from difficult to impossible. The nature of dancing in the entertainment field is so sporadic and unsure. Look at a typical hard working dance career.

You work a show in Los Angeles for six weeks but it closes because the backers pulled out. You don't work for a week. You pick up two days work on a music video. You don't work for two weeks. You finally land a job that takes you to Japan for two months. Another two weeks unemployed. Get the picture! When you're trying to explain that type of career to a loan officer at a bank, they stare at you as if you were asking them to finance the space shuttle. One of the great benefits to working a Las Vegas production show is longevity. Some of these shows have been running continuously for twenty years, and although they go through various changes or "editions", if you're good you can be assured of working long enough to establish a good credit rating. There is no other place in the States where you'll find more dancers working continuously for five to ten years and buying new cars and nice homes on credit. Some long time Vegas dancers feel they may have compromised some things in their career by working Vegas, but this type of lifestyle has more than made up for it.

HOUSING AND COST OF LIVING

Las Vegas is growing rapidly, and construction of apartments and housing is keeping pace with this rapid growth. This boom in construction has helped

keep the cost of housing in Vegas relatively low in
comparison to N.Y. or L.A. Let me give you a very
general example of housing costs in the three cities.
In L.A. a one bedroom apartment in a good
neighborhood will run about $650 a month, in NYC
somewhere around $1,100 and in Vegas with pool,
jacuzzi, and cable TV, $400–$450 a month. Again,
this is just an example and you can get great deals
everywhere, if you're lucky and diligent. The point
is that housing, both renting or buying is far less in
Vegas than in the Big Apple or the Big Orange and
that is something to think about.

Food is another example. Though I haven't
noticed any real differences in the supermarkets, the
casinos are always enticing people to gamble by
offering some of the best prices on food you will ever
see. Complete breakfast buffets for $.49, and it's not
surprising to have a huge prime rib dinner for $3.95.
Gawd, this sounds like a commercial, but I want you
to have as much insight as possible when you're
making career decisions.

But this is not a travelogue. The purpose of this
book is to inform accurately both sides, good and
bad.

If you have a compulsive personality or if
moderation is a word that you're not familiar with,
Las Vegas can be a disaster area. Gambling is
everywhere, twenty–four hours a day, everyday of
the year. It's exciting, it's fun, and it's glamourized
heavily by the corporations who own the casino
resorts. I've had friends get into serious financial
trouble gambling. They cash their paycheck, and
proceed to spend it all that night, gambling. The

next morning they need to borrow money for rent, bills or food. Oh sure, some people do win lots of money, but the truth is, they've built a very large city on the losers. For the vacationer who loses some money and returns home this is not a problem. But for the compulsive local who has the ability to gamble everyday of his life, this can be frightening. It can be far worse than a drug problem, because it's legal.

Ahhh, speaking of drug problems. I know that drugs exist everywhere and believe me this is not a sermon, but for some reason, maybe the late hours, or the party atmosphere, drugs seem to be more prevalent in the back stage areas of Vegas than in other shows in other cities. The drugs backstage seem to rise and fall in cycles depending on the people working the shows, but I do remember a couple of instances where it got so bad the local police set up a sting operation with hidden cameras in the backstage bathrooms. Alcohol is also more prevalent in Las Vegas. You say how can that be? Well, anytime you're gambling in a casino, you drink free. If you gamble all night, and many people do, you drink free all night. Another difference is, in most towns the bars close at 1 or 2 AM, but in Vegas there is a small tavern on almost every corner and they don't know the meaning of the word "closed".

I mentioned in the beginning of this chapter that I would try to discuss both sides and let you ultimately decide if Vegas is for you. The truth is, if you're a career minded dancer with common sense and some restraint, then Las Vegas is a great place to live and work.

CLASS

Another benefit to working in Las Vegas is the abundance of quality instructors in a variety of dance classes. Don't take this for granted. On a cruise ship or in a foreign show it's very difficult to take class, but in Las Vegas you can keep up your technique, learn new styles, and become a better dancer while you're working. The dance class is the lifeline of the dancer, and as discussed earlier, dance class for the professional is invaluable. Every dancer knows how important class is to their dance abilities, but learning the styles of established and up and coming choreographers who teach class is equally as important. A choreographer is holding an audition and he recognizes you from his class. You already have an advantage in the fact that he knows you study, that you're hard working and you're capable of performing his style of dance.

THE BILLBOARD

The billboard of a dance studio is the number one place for finding new work. If I'm producing a show the first place I post the audition information is on the billboard of a dance studio. Why? I want dancers who are studying and sharp, and the word of mouth is going to insure a good turnout. The billboard with audition information reinforces the benefits of working in a job where you can take class. Don't follow me? Look!

Every dancer knows the benefits of dance class:

To keep technique sharp;

To learn new styles of dance from different
teachers;

To hear about auditions for dance jobs.

These benefits are important to your career as a dancer. In fact, I want you to think of your ability to take class as a positive or negative when you consider accepting a certain type of dance job. Example: you're working on a cruise ship and although you're having a good time and making decent money, the chances of you taking class are minimal. But let's say the cast is very career minded and one of the more experienced dancers decides to give everyone a good workout. This is great! You'll keep your technique sharp, but because the ship is so isolated from the dance world, it's very difficult to set up your next job while working.

Consider dance class to be another benefit to working in Las Vegas. Vegas has many quality studios with terrific teachers, but the point is you'll be able to audition for other dance jobs while working. Everyone knows it's always easier to get a job when you already have a job. Many dance troupes and Broadway tours come through Las Vegas and you'll be able to audition for these higher paying jobs. Many dancers have landed Broadway shows from Las Vegas, myself included.

In summation, I feel class in Las Vegas is clearly a plus. To make studying easier, here are a list of dance studios complete with addresses and phone numbers.

Backstage Studios
1952½ E. Sahara
457–7310

Dance West
4133 W. Charleston
870–5508

Simba Studios
3021 Valley View
367–6788

Rainbow School of Dance
21 N. Mojave Road
384–6268

Maliza's Studios
4133 W. Charleston
870–5508

Academy of Nevada Dance
4634 S. Maryland Parkway
798–2989

Helen Gregory
Talent Center
3755 E. Desert Inn Road
451–1666

UNLV Dept. of Dance
739–3827

Talent Unlimited
3401 Sirius
871–3999

Las Vegas Dance Theatre
3248 Civic Center Drive
649–3932

Fern Adair Conservatory
3265 E. Patrick
458–7575

Farrington Agency
4350 Arville
362–3000

Centerstage
5013 Alta Drive
878–7994

London Dance Academy
4000 Boulder Highway
456–5334

Wonderland School
of Dance
3430 E. Tropicana
456–6668

LAS VEGAS PRODUCTIONS

You can submit pictures and resumés to these Entertainment Directors.

Aladdin Hotel
3367 Las Vegas Blvd.
Las Vegas, NV 89109
(702) 736-0111
Entertainment Director:
Jim Barnes
"Country Tonite"

Harrah's
3475 Las Vegas Blvd.
Las Vegas, NV 89109
(702) 369-5000
Entertainment Director:
Dick Foster
"Spellbound"

Arizona Charlie's
740 South Decatur
Las Vegas, NV 89107
(702) 258-5200
Entertainment Director:
Joe Guercio
Penny France's "Saddle"

Imperial Palace
3575 Las Vegas Blvd.
Las Vegas, NV 89109
(702) 731-3311
Entertainment Director:
John Stuarts
"Legends in Concert"

Bally's
3645 Las Vegas Blvd.
Las Vegas, NV 89109
(702) 739-4111
Entertainment Director:
Joel Fishman
"Jubilee"

Mirage
3400 Las Vegas Blvd.
Las Vegas, NV 89109
(702) 791-1111
Entertainment Director:
Todd Dougal
"Siegfried & Roy"

Hacienda
2535 Las Vegas Blvd.
Las Vegas, NV 89109
(702) 739-8911
Entertainment Director:
Ron Andrews
"Lance Burton"

Riviera
2901 Las Vegas Blvd.
Las Vegas, NV 89109
(702) 734-5110
Entertainment Director:
Barbara Hayes
"Splash"

Tropicana
3801 Las Vegas Blvd.
Las Vegas, NV 89109
(702) 729-2222
Entertainment Director:
Larry Lee
"Folies Bergere"

The Rio
3700 W. Flamingo
Las Vegas, NV 89109
(702) 252-7777
Entertainment Director:
Lyn Baxter
"Brazilia"

Stardust
3000 Las Vegas Blvd.
Las Vegas, NV 89109
(702) 732-6111
Entertainment Director:
Ted Lorenz
"Enter the Night"

CHAPTER SEVEN

MTV/MUSIC VIDEO

Talking with Michael Peters about dance is like plugging your Sony Walkman into Hoover Dam. He is a well known dancer/director/choreographer who's having the kind of career three people would be satisfied with. Later in the interview, Michael talks about the importance of being a versatile dancer. Recapping his career only demonstrates the advice he gives to young dancers, "Versatility parallels success — don't limit yourself."

Michael Peters never limited himself; directing film and television, directing and choreographing theatre, conceiving and staging night clubs acts for big name entertainers and working as a dancer all over the world. I'm not kidding, the list just goes on and on.

With all this work, Michael is still best known for something else... Music Video. During our interview he had to laugh, "I've choreographed Broadway, film and television and there are people out there who think all I do is choreograph music videos."

There's a good reason for this. Here's a partial list of the music videos with a Peters touch:

Michael Jackson	*Beat It*
	Thriller
Billy Joel	*Uptown Girl*
Pat Benetar	*Love is a Battlefield*
Diana Ross	*Pieces of Ice*
Lionel Ritchie	*Dancing on the Ceiling*
	Hello
	Ballerina
	Say You, Say Me
	Running with the Night

Let's go to the beginning. Michael Peters broke new ground in music video by choreographing Michael Jackson's hit, "BEAT IT". "BEAT IT" was the first time a group of dancers got to use the art of dance to help promote a record release in the video market.

Early on, "BEAT IT" helped to open a new area of work for dancers and expose a massive audience to dance. Sounds great, doesn't it? But music video is not without its problems. Most of these problems still exist today.

DM: *Tell me a little bit about the early days of "BEAT IT" and "THRILLER."*

_MP: Well, it was exciting. We had a large group of dancers and its always exciting to have a lot of dancers creating, dancers playing, dancers making money.

DM: *Do you remember what they made?*

MP: I always try to make sure that my dancers make around $250 a day. Sometimes they'll get $1,000 for the week, which is good. I don't remember exactly what they made, but I'm sure it was something like that. You have to remember "BEAT IT" had a budget of $165,000 in 1982. This was a lot of money. "THRILLER" was even more, just over a million and again the dancers were well taken care of. The big difference between then and now is budget. The record companies today want to make videos for 50–60 thousand. They just don't want to pay. There's no money in it for me or the dancers, which is why I don't do them anymore.

DM: *So there really hasn't been the enormous amount of work available for dancers?*

MP: Well, for a while, in the beginning, maybe. Here's what happened. On a particular video I was working on, I found out the producers were going to make and market "the making of" this music video. That's where they show the behind the scenes action of what went into this video. Kind of like the making of "Indiana Jones" or something. The dancers were hired to do the video and I was hired to choreograph the video, but "the making of" this video is a separate project and I told the producers they would have to negotiate with the dancers. Well, it was a two day shoot and on the second day, they still hadn't negotiated with the kids, so I threatened to pull the dancers off the set and was going to walk off myself. Well, we had a meeting. The producers told us that if they do "the making of" and if they show it anywhere, they would abide by any union rules for payment. Then they very cleverly drew up little contracts stating just that. Everyone signed and returned to work. About two months later when the video and "the making of" were showing everywhere, we called SAG (Screen Actors Guild). SAG told us they didn't have any jurisdiction in that department. They still don't today. There isn't a union covering any music videos and the producers knew that. Because there aren't any minimums, membership or guidelines, anyone's aunt, cousin or sister who ever had one dance lesson in their life is now "a dancer". With competition so great, producers will get someone for $70 a day instead of $250. Now remember, without guidelines we're talking 14–16 hour days, no overtime, no benefits... nothing. You're just on the set till the video's finished. The well trained dancer won't work that way, so what started out as a boom to good dancers work–wise, really isn't worthwhile anymore.

DM: *But you worked with big names.*

MP: Yes, fortunately, I worked with big name entertainers who wanted quality and I could demand certain things. The last video I did was with Lionel Ritchie and the dancers were paid $1,000 for 4 or 5 days, but I could watch the number of hours we worked, make sure dancers got breaks, you know, take care of dancers needs.

DM: *So again, a dancers lifeline is the choreographer.*

MP: Always.

DM: *Give me a quick good side, bad side to music videos.*

MP: There still is some good work out there. Janet Jackson uses dancers and pays well. Paula Abdul and Madonna use dancers and do quality work.   Unfortunately, they're the exception. Bad side, there are no benefits. If you get hurt on the set, break an ankle or something, it's over. You might get the initial accident taken care of, but you'll be out of the video and won't be paid for the two or three months you can't dance — it's over! It's a big risk to take for $70 a day.

DM: *What about the ethnic street dancers?*

MP: What "BEAT IT" did in the beginning for the trained dancer in terms of work, music videos are still doing for the street dancer. Right now, hip–hop is in. I have two projects right now using these hip–hop street dancers. The problem is, hip–hop is limited in terms of choreography and these kids don't do anything else. They don't tap or ballet. But hip–hop is hot right now, especially in music videos. The funny thing is, trained dancers have spent thousands of dollars on ballet and tap and some producers will say "Can you do hip–hop?" But its all cyclical.

DM: *A trained dancer will always work.*

MP: Always!

DM: *Should a trained dancer do a music video?*

MP: Yes! If you've never done a video and you get one. If it's a big name video and it pays well and you get some exposure—I mean, if it's on MTV. If it's not on MTV it'll be very limited in terms of exposure. If that's the case, then I say maybe you shouldn't do it.

DM: *What about an audition? What do you want in a dancer? Let's say you're going to cast a video tomorrow. What do you want in terms of look, attitude, technique, everything?*

MP: Yes, everything. All of that. I can't speak for other people, but from what I see of their work, certainly Paula Abdul, Vince Patterson and myself! The people that are working a lot right now are still from the old school, where you better have ballet technique and you better have jazz training. I mean, look at Paula, she's using tap in her videos. I'm really big on technique and my stuff is very rhythmic, so people have to have a good musicality, a good sense of rhythm. What I always look for — doesn't matter what the job is — I love individuals. I love people with personalities different from everyone else. See, I came in on the fringe of Broadway shows where <u>you had to look like everyone else.</u> I hated it, because that's not why I was in this business. I am in this business because its a creative art form. It's about what my personality can bring to something. So that's what I look for. I love individuals who have their own specific look and personality.

DM: *What are young dancers lacking?*

MP: I find, a lot of young dancers specialize. They say "I only do... this or... that." I think that's very limiting because ultimately, everything is cyclical, you should try to do everything.

DM: *That's true!   The dancers that are more versatile work.*

MP: Yes, that's why when you look at the major music videos today you see a lot of the same kids.

DM: *Are you going to cast differently for Lionel Ritchie than Madonna?*

MP: Absolutely. That's a good example. Lionel is older and reaches a different market. You don't want to put babies with him. I mean, if Lionel is going to dance with a woman you want him to dance with a woman, not a child. Madonna is definitely catering to a teenage market. I went to a run through the other day for her tour, and the oldest person in there was 25, maybe 28.

DM: *How much of your casting is done on the phone?*

MP: Sometimes I'll call people and cast everyone. Like "THRILLER." I called everybody on the phone and hired them. I called the sickest people I knew! Really! I told them we're doing this project where you're going to be in the most bizarre make–up for two days straight. Your mothers won't recognize you, but if you want to come and play, come on. I like to try to have new kids each time, I think its important, but you have to have a core of dancers who know your style. That's important, too. Again, a lot of the new kids today are limited. A young dancer has to watch the type of class they're taking and make sure they're getting some good training. A lot of classes today are just dance combinations. They warm up for ten minutes and do a combination, that's it. No body positions, no developing, no corrections, and a hot class just consists of a hot combination. You've got classes today like "cardio–funk class". What is that? I'll never forget when we were auditioning for "Dreamgirls". I wanted to do every step I ever knew for this audition, right? Bob Avion, a co–choreographer is sitting in the theater and I'm up there on stage dancing hard, doing this long combination. So I come down into the audience, sit next to him and he says, 'Darling, just give them, second, open fourth, double pirouette, close fifth front.   If they can't do that, they can't dance. Stop wasting your time, my time and their time.' That's the truth!

Update !

Dance Alliance Helps Get Minimums For Music Videos!

Dance Alliance is a committee of dancers who got together on their own to represent agent–represented dancers as well as non–represented dancers. They've formed an alliance to establish some guidelines for the dance community to live by. In the area of music videos they've been very successful. They've established minimums, overtime, hazard pay, all sorts of things—guidelines that didn't exist until now. The minimum wage for a 12 hour day in music video is now $275 per day and will be increasing in the near future.

If we work together, it will get better.

CHAPTER EIGHT

THE DANCE AGENT

Yes, they exist, and they can help a dancer mold a career. Let me tell what I've learned about dance agents, and again, let you decide if this is right for you. As far as I know, Los Angeles is the only city with agents representing only dancers. If you know of a true dance agent in another city please write and let me know. At this time there are four dance agents in the L.A. area.

First of all, I feel dance agents provide a full service to the dancers they represent but you should know that both represented dancers and non-represented dancers can have terrific dance careers. I found it interesting that many of the older dancers are uncomfortable with a dance agent. They like going to an open call, advertised in the trades, where everyone shows up and the best dancers win. On the other side many dancers like being represented by someone who knows the business, can negotiate a deal, help if something goes wrong and submit them for dance jobs where the competition is more selective but the numbers are

far less.   No matter how you feel, dance agents in
L.A. are here to stay and have changed the dance
market.   I wouldn't be surprised if dance agents
started popping up all over the states. I know as an
actor I may not always like how the game is played,
but I know I can't win if I don't play.

A downside to the emergence of dance agents is
to the non–represented dancer. A producer calls a
dance agent directly and allows them to submit 20 or
30 dancers for their new project.   The
non–represented dancer never hears about the
project.

In fairness, dance agents are bringing a
respectability to the dance market and helping to
solve many problems dancers have faced for a long
time.

I interviewed Julie McDonald. Julie is head of the
dance department for Joseph, Heldfond and Rix.
Joseph, Heldfond and Rix is a major commercial
agent and Julie handles dancers for commercials,
film, TV, Equity and a variety of other jobs. Julie is
without a doubt a pioneer in the dance field, but too
modest to say so. She has been in business for eight
years and has weathered much of the cynicism and
animosity that comes with breaking into this field.

JM: I did have resistance in the beginning.
Resistance from older dancers who were used
to working a certain way. Resistance from
choreographers who were threatened, and
resistance from some in the industry who
didn't take dance seriously. But to tell you the

truth, it really took off like wildfire. I continue to get some resistance but many choreographers see now that we provide a service for them. We can provide them with dancers they wouldn't see otherwise. We've taken a lot of the burden off choreographers who had to provide producers with dancers. Choreographers have traditionally negotiated for dancers. Well, this is crazy! I mean, directors don't negotiate for actors. Why should choreographers negotiate for dancers.

DM: *Tell me about Dance Alliance.*

JM: Dance Alliance is a committee of dancers who got together on their own and represent agent–represented dancers and non–represented dancers. They've formed an alliance to create some guidelines for the dance community to live and work by—primarily in the area of Music Videos, where they've been very successful. They've established with the music industry, minimums, overtime pay, hazard pay, all sorts of things where there were no guidelines previously. Minimum pay for a twelve hour work day in the field of music video is now $275 and will be increasing in the near future. Now, they'll try to set some guidelines for industrials, especially non–union industrials which are plentiful out here. So that's next.

DM: *That's great. I want dancers to know things like that.*

JM: Yes, its good there are minimums now, but dancers should also know there's not enough work anymore. From 1988 – 1990, those three years, you could make a living from music videos. No kidding, you could <u>pay your rent</u>. But not anymore, the music industry does not have the big budget for music videos any more. Maybe Michael Jackson or Janet or Paula Abdul, but even then the budgets are reduced.

DM: *OK. I want Julie McDonald to represent me. What do I do?*

JM: Call. We will tell everyone the same thing. Send in a picture and resumé. You should have at least that much—but say you don't. You can send in a Polaroid so at least we know what you look like. Send some kind of resumé, even if it doesn't have professional work on it. Put your training on it, your high school work, your college work. Something. We'll give you an audition, here in L.A. You realize you can't work if you don't relocate to New York or L.A. Possibly Chicago or San Francisco.

DM: *With all these dancers submitting, I'm sure you have to be selective.*

JM: We have to be very selective. My agency will do the preliminaries through pictures and resumés. Then we'll invite them to an audition.

DM: *What type of dancer?*

JM: All types! I'm a full service agency. Some dancers may just move well but have a great commercial look. I will represent them for commercials. Another may be a great technician but I can't represent them for commercials. I'll represent them for everything else. Another dancer may have a great legit resumé, they're terrific in equity type shows. I represent all types.

DM: *Tell me about the audition.*

JM: It's run by local choreographers, working choreographers, and it's run like a class. Like the combination of a class and a typical audition. So I not only look at how they dance and how they look, but I also see how they audition. Auditioning for me is no different then auditioning for a producer. I watch how fast they pick up, what their attitude is like. How they look when they audition, all these things.

DM: *What about how they look, meaning what should they wear?*

JM: We give people guidelines on what to wear if they're novices. They should know the right questions to ask. What do I wear? That's a good question, but everyone should know that they should try to look good. We might want to change their look after we sign them. They may not look like what's really selling out here. But everyone should try to look nice.

DM: *So does that mean heels and full makeup for women?*

JM: NO! No longer. Everything is so individualized. It means, you have to look the best you can look as an individual. Some people need full makeup, others have a look that's a natural look. Say it's a traditional TV special like a Bob Hope Special, yes, you need full makeup and heels, but if it's a fly–girl, no way. They want you to wear your combat boots. If you don't look like that you won't get in the front door. You have to know the project.

DM: *All right, they've been through the audition. You select how many?*

JM: A few... really! We bring in around sixty people, we audition four times a year and each time we may take six people. But that's not the only way to get in. I have scouts out watching classes. Sometimes I hear someone is wonderful. I'll ask them to take class with a choreographer and may stop by and take a look.

DM: *Great! I always stress class, not just for training, but for careers.*

JM: So do I.

DM: *I've noticed with three dance agents in L.A., auditions in the trades have declined.*

JM: Yes.

DM: *Do you think that hurts the dancers that don't have an agent?*

JM: Yes.

DM: *So now it's even more competitive.*

JM: Yes! And work has changed dramatically. There's not an abundance of work right now and there are a million dancers out there. I think a dancer must positively want to dance. You have to have the right psychological makeup to succeed. I think dancing is for everybody. Having a career as a dancer is not. Dancing for self expression, for the joy, for the way it makes you feel, should not be discouraged. You can take your dance to other areas, education, dance therapy... whatever. But a professional dancer! You've got to have the right everything! If you want to be a dancer you can't just be a dancer. You have to sing, act, do gymnastics, martial arts, roller–blading. It's never ending and it changes all the time.

DM: *Tell me some recourses a dancer with you has that a dancer without representation doesn't have.*

JM: Well, if we do it right, I have leverage, but I'm in a situation right now where a choreographer hired dancers, represented dancers, without notifying me. The dancers were promised a certain amount of money and after 3 weeks rehearsal, they didn't receive what they were promised. So they call me and want me to help. Well, at this point, I have very little leverage and I'm just trying to patch up the holes. But they're stuck. Stuck! This is what an agent can help avoid.

DM: *What is it you want the dancer to know about what you can do for them.*

JM: I want them to know in my working for them I can give them career guidance, I will negotiate everything for them and I give them protection against nonpayment or not fulfilling the contract negotiated. The other thing I want them to know is they will be submitted for dance jobs in film, TV and equity stage. Jobs they would otherwise not hear about.

DANCE AGENTS

Here is information on the dance agents currently working in the L.A. area.

Joseph, Heldfond & Rix
Attn: Julie McDonald
1717 N. Highland Ave., Suite 414
Hollywood, CA 90028
(213) 466-9111

Bobby Ball Talent Agency
Attn: Teresa Taylor or Susan Salgado
8075 W. 3rd St., Suite 550
Los Angeles, CA 90048
(213) 964-7300

Victor Kruglov & Associates
8282 Sunset Blvd.
Los Angeles, CA 90046
(213) 848-3445

L.A. Talent Agency
Attn: Tim O'Brien
8335 Sunset Blvd.
Los Angeles, CA 90069
(213) 656-3722

CHAPTER NINE

WHERE'S THE BALLET?

Can you talk about the history of literature without mentioning Shakespeare? Can you explain how languages developed and not mention Latin? And yet, here I am writing about career possibilities for dancers, and I haven't discussed ballet companies. I've agonized about this section for months. When I first began researching ballet I realized I was going to have a problem. There are hundreds of ballet companies nationwide. The number of companies isn't as frightening as the diversity. There are professional or union companies, secondary and regional ballet companies. Universities have companies, civic ballets and even large dance schools form their own ballet companies. To truly do ballet justice, I would need to write a whole book on the subject. Really! There are so many differences in terms of scholarships, pay, performances, rehearsals and class. To discuss these differences would not be practical. Let me show you why. The focus of this book is to inform about non–union work that young dancers will find easier to get when they're starting out, but when it comes to ballet companies, the secondary companies are just too different. Some companies pay, some don't. Most companies give you training and the opportunity to perform in lieu of money.

Some secondary companies hire professional dancers seasonally with a troupe of non–professional in the corps. The variations are staggering!

Another problem is longevity. In Europe, many ballet companies are subsidized by their government. In the U.S., ballet companies have to apply for grants and hope for private donations. As our government reduces the amount of money available to the arts, many companies have been hit hard. I found a reference book listing smaller ballet companies. It was written in 1987, and almost 40% of the companies listed are not performing today.

Now don't get depressed. There are new companies forming all the time and ballet will always be around, but from a research point of view, the rapidity of change makes some information obsolete before it gets to print.

Last reason: I've covered many topics I feel have been neglected by other authors, but ballet has been covered extensively, and information about ballet companies is all around you. I'm going to take a gamble and say that I'll bet I can find a dance school in the U.S. that doesn't have any knowledge of what a dancer's life is like in a Japanese production.

I'd also be willing to wager that there isn't a qualified dance studio in the U.S. that doesn't have an abundance of information about nearby ballet companies and probably has contacts there. It stands to reason that teachers know about ballet companies, most dance teachers have performed in professional and secondary companies. But—how many dance teachers across the U.S. have danced in Music Videos. Really, information about local, regional and professional ballet companies is as close as a subscription to Dance Magazine. They interview ballet masters, artistic directors and teachers. They share tips, new techniques, and even advertisements from ballet companies that are announcing auditions and granting scholarships. They even have a ten page list of schools, teachers and regional companies broken down state by state.

But I'm not going to wimp out on ballet dancers!

I've decided to once again give you an example of what the best is offering and allow you to judge all other companies accordingly.

I contacted AGMA (The American Guild of Musical Artists). AGMA is the guild representing professional ballet companies. AGMA not only covers dancers but Apprentices, Narrators, Singers, choreographers, stage managers and stage directors. AGMA has a fifty page National Dance Basic Agreement, but don't worry. I'll just give you the highlights of the agreement.

BONDS

Bonds are just one way AGMA protects the ballet dancer. A professional dance company must put up a bond at least one week before any rehearsal, engagement or any travel to an engagement may take place. The security bond will be paid by the Employer to AGMA. If the ballet company is an established company the bond will be one week's salary for the members of the company. If a ballet company suddenly folded, the dancers would receive their last week's check.

COMPENSATION

Minimum compensation – Rehearsal/Performance   weeks

Apprentice	227.50
New Dancer	455.00
Corps Dancer	575.00
Solo Dancer	625.00
Principal Dancer	680.00

It doesn't stop there. Professional Ballet companies have negotiated:

Overtime pay – an hourly rate of around $30 payable in one–half hour increments.

Travel overtime – an hourly rate of around $20 payable in one–half hour increments if your travel happens to take longer than expected or you're forced to travel on what would normally be your free day.

Extraordinary Risk Pay – a rate of $40 for each on–stage technical rehearsal, dress rehearsal and each performance that a dancer performs four feet above the stage, suspended from a wire or on stilts or ramps.

Per Diem – will be paid to any dancer required to be more than 30 miles from the in–city departure point. Per Diem is around $40.

REHEARSAL

A rehearsal week shall mean a Monday through Sunday week. It will consist of five rehearsal days and two free days. Rehearsal weeks do not need to be consecutive.

Other rehearsals can include:

Emergency rehearsal – a rehearsal necessitated by the inability of a dancer to perform due to sickness or injury.

Spill–over rehearsals – which means an unscheduled rehearsal of the same ballet. Spill–over rehearsal shall not exceed one–half hour per day.

Dress Rehearsal – a rehearsal which includes the following elements:

1. All performing Artists shall appear in full costume and makeup.

2. All scenery, lighting, props and costumes are utilized.

3. Full orchestra utilized.

4. No printed program or program credits.

PERFORMANCE

The Artist may be required to take part in not more than seven performances per week on tour and not more than eight performances per week in the city of origination.

A demonstration shall count as one–half performance providing that the total elapsed time including travel does not exceed 4 hours and that each demonstration does not exceed 50 minutes. If you perform back to back demonstrations they must not exceed 50 minutes and must have a rest period of 25 minutes between. It's equivalent to one full performance.

The following topics and many others have been negotiated and agreed upon by producers and AGMA:

Travel – Bus, Air or Train

Hotels

Photographic calls

Seniority

Royalties

Costume fittings

Medical benefits

Master classes

The Guild has left nothing to chance when it comes to protecting the ballet dancer. Whether you've just been hired to perform with ABT, dance in the corps of a regional ballet company or dance

locally just for the fun of it, you should be aware of
AGMA's basic dance agreement to protect dancers.

AGMA

1727 Broadway, Second Floor
New York City, NY 10019-5284
(212) 265-3687

CHAPTER TEN

WHY THE UNIONS?

I have discussed non–union work throughout this book for two reasons. 1) Most young dancers will find non–union work easier to get while they're gaining experience and establishing a resumé. 2) Non–union work has the potential for more of the pitfalls discussed in the book, since guidelines and minimums haven't been established and recourse against a producer is difficult.

So what are the benefits to performing union work and why should a dancer strive to be in the union?

RESPECTABILITY

If you're a union dancer, everyone knows you've danced on commercials, TV specials, film or in Equity stage productions. A producer or director will immediately see your union affiliations at the top of your resumé and know you have experience at the union level. You'll also enjoy the benefit of being able to audition first for other union work.

Example: A Broadway production will audition all Equity dancers first. Only if the producer can't find what he's looking for from the union pool of dancers will he look at non–union dancers.

RECOURSE

As discussed briefly in "Where's the Ballet?", a union will require a producer to put up a bond. A bond is a sum of money held by the union to insure the dancer of *some* payment. The bond is usually equivalent to one week's salary of the cast. If a producer closes the production and doesn't pay the dancers, the bond will be forfeited by the producer and dispensed to the dancers. In the days before the unions, the dancers would not only be out the last week's check, but if they were on the road, they'd have to find a way to get home.

Another, more serious type of recourse is litigation. A non–union dancer that has not received payment will find it difficult and expensive to try to sue a producer. The Guild has lawyers on staff that will attempt to litigate for union members. I said attempt because even union lawyers have a difficult time.

HORROR STORY!

Let's say, I'm going to produce a play in San Diego. I form "Green Eyes Production Co.", and produce the show. A month into the run, ticket sales are not going well. I am unable to pay back investors. I owe dancers, actors, crews, the theater, advertisers, everybody! I close the show. Green Eyes Productions declares bankruptcy, dissolves, and is difficult to sue. Three months later, I open Blue Eyes Productions and try again.

THAT'S SHOW BIZ!

These production companies are earmarked in the membership magazine.

When you're hired by a production company, and it's a union job, call the union and ask if the production company is in good standing with the union.

NEGOTIATED MINIMUMS

The Guilds have negotiated minimums for every job covered under their jurisdiction. If you're working in a dinner theater with 300 seats, or a Broadway show with 1700 seats, there are minimum salaries that cannot be violated. You'll hear minimums referred to as "scale". The unions will not let scale payment to the performer be violated, which is how the phrase "scale plus ten" came about. A producer will have to pay scale *plus* the extra ten percent for agent fees. The minimum salaries generally increase a small amount annually. Some dancers scoff at these small increases, but if you remember "Foreign Productions – Mexico," salaries for at least ten productions spanning a period of eight years, remained at the same level.

MEDICAL BENEFITS

Equity, AFTRA and SAG have medical and dental plans for qualifying members. I have qualified for and utilized SAG and AFTRA plans. Believe me, they have quality plans that sure help when you have an emergency. The problem is, like all insurance policies, they've gotten more and more expensive. Hospital fees, doctor fees and the onslaught of the Aids epidemic have taken a toll on union insurance policies. Not too long ago, an AFTRA member had to earn $2,000 in a year to qualify for medical and dental benefits for the member and their family. Today, that number is $7,500, and the dental plan for spouses and children has been dropped completely. Equity (the stage union), also hard hit, has increased the number of weeks you'll need to work before you're eligible for benefits. SAG has maintained their medical and dental policies, but the eligibility minimums continue to rise. Minimums are $7,500 now with rumors of $10,000 soon.

PENSIONS

The unions have created pension funds for members. Can you imagine, a dancer with a retirement fund! The producers have agreed to pay a percentage of moneys paid in salary into the members' pension fund. If a member earns a certain amount of money in a year, the union considers that one qualifying year. Right now, a member needs ten qualifying years to become vested and receive a minimum pension after age 55, (early retirement). Of course, if you have larger salaries during qualifying years, or more than ten qualifying years, your pension will increase accordingly.

RESIDUALS

Without a doubt, one of my favorite topics. Once you receive your first residual payment, it'll be your favorite, too. You never really know when a residual is coming, so its always a little surprise from heaven.

Residuals are not a gift and did not come about without a fight. I think you should know a little bit about the history of residuals. In 1971, the Guild felt it wasn't fair for producers to reuse programming again and again without compensating the Guild member. After a difficult negotiation process, residuals began in 1974. In 1979, the cable field was emerging, and producers found residual payments to once again be a priority with the Guild. Unable to reach what the Guild felt was fair, they voted to strike. The SAG strike lasted four months from July 21 to October 23.

The sacrifices other Guild members made in the past allow us to enjoy today's residuals.

Here's a very simplistic explanation of how residuals happen and how the Guild monitors them.

For a network television show rerun on network television, you will receive a percentage of your original salary. Each time the show is played the percentage will decrease. I just received a residual payment of $64.00 for a television program I worked on over _eight_ years ago. Commercial residuals are similar with one exception. A national commercial will pay a certain amount for the original shoot, and like a television show, your residual percentage will decrease as your commercial is rerun. Unlike television shows, after a 13 week period, if your commercial is <u>picked</u> <u>up</u> (or bought again), the residual percentage will again start at the top. The other difference between a television show and a commercial, is your commercial will likely run on all three networks, giving you a greater potential for many more residuals. So, how does the Guild keep track of every member's residual payment. When a sponsor purchases air time to show their commercial, they must also pay the actors who performed in that spot. The Guild receives lists of all commercial air time purchased on any given day.

For film, it's a little more difficult. If you perform in a made for TV movie, the residual payment is similar to a television show. If you perform in a film shown at the movie theater and later shown on TV (e.g., "Lethal Weapon"), the network producers purchase the film for a certain amount of money. The actors collectively receive 2% of this purchase price. That 2% is then paid to the actors according to how much they made on the original shoot. Example: an actor making $10,000 on the original shoot will get a higher percentage than an actor making $7,500.

Again, this is an over–simplified explanation of how the union monitors residuals, but it should give some insight into the process.

OTHER BENEFITS

There are many other benefits to being a member of the unions and I'll briefly mention some of them.

Credit Union – You can join the AFTRA–SAG or Equity credit union and establish checking accounts, savings accounts, credit cards, ATM cards, or apply for low–interest home, car or personal loans.

Hotlines – The Guilds have established hotlines that you can call to receive information on auditions, meetings or current Guild proceedings.

Agents – There is an indirect but important benefit to dancers becoming union members in terms of getting an agent. Many dancers cross over into acting and having union affiliation makes it a little easier to get seen by agents. Many SAG–franchised agents will not see anyone that doesn't possess a SAG card.

Classes and Showcases – You can sign up for a special class or seminar given by the Guild for its members. There are also showcase nights, where you can prepare a scene for working casting directors.

Every dancer should strive for union affiliation. Union affiliation gives you credibility, many benefits and the opportunity to audition for the best work available to dancers.

JOINING A UNION

The following information explains how you can join the unions, what membership fees are, and how current dues are calculated.

SAG

Membership Fee: $1,012.50

Union Dues: – depend on previous year earnings. Minimum is $85 a year for earning
0 – 5,000 dollars

How to Join: – You must perform union work prior to joining. Call for appointment.
L.A. (213) 456–4000   N.Y. (212) 944–1030

AFTRA

Membership Fee: $800.00

Union Dues: $42.50 every six months.

How to Join: AFTRA is an open union. You do not need to perform union work prior to being able to join. You'll need to go to an AFTRA office, fill out an application, and pay initial fees and first 6 month dues for a total of $842.50

Equity

Membership Fee: $800.00

Union Dues: $39.00 every six months. If you joined SAG or AFTRA first (your parent union) and you are current with them, Equity gives you a five dollar break on dues, or $34.00 every 6 months.

How to Join: Equity has two different ways to join.

1) If you're hired to perform an Equity production, bring your contract to Equity and apply. A major benefit to joining this way is, Equity will take part of your salary weekly and you won't have to pay all the fees up—front.

2) If your Parent union is SAG and you've made a certain amount of money in a certain year, you are eligible to join Equity if you choose. This specific monetary amount increases each year; $1348 in 1992, $1428 in 1993, etc. Also, if you join using #2 you will have to pay all membership fees when you apply.

Chapter Eleven

SUMMARY

It's difficult to put life experiences into information a dancer can use, but I feel any dancer reading this book can see the common threads that every choreographer, Entertainment Director and dance agent find invaluable.

CLASS AND TRAINING

<u>Everyone</u> stresses the importance of training. If you're living in your home town and thinking about relocating to N.Y. or LA, please take their advice to heart. Get the best training you can possibly get. After you relocate, everyone agrees that taking class is the only way to survive. It will keep you sharp, help you learn new styles and it's where you'll make most of your connections. If you're thinking you can get by with the training you have – Forget it! Not only is the competition severe, but the people holding the auditions can spot a well trained dancer in a count of eight.

VERSATILITY

In today's entertainment market, is anything more important? Remember Michael Peters' advice, "Don't limit yourself." A versatile dancer is a hot commodity. If you're a street dancer, add some technique training. If you're a classically trained dancer, work on vocals. You never know when you're going to need it. I've had to roller skate in industrials and perform stunt fighting in a Vegas revue. Versatility is a key to making money. Everyone agrees, don't limit yourself.

ATTITUDE

Who trains for that! It comes from knowing who you are, what you want and treating others with respect. You've heard everyone interviewed say you'll be evaluated on your attitude as much as your dance ability, sometimes more. Attitude is not only how you treat your employers, but how you treat other dancers. I told you earlier dancers love to talk and the dance community is very small. I remember dancing in a show where the producers called a meeting and asked the cast about a particular dancer they were considering. Over half the cast had worked with this dancer before, found her difficult to work with and asked the producers not to hire her. She was never hired. Attitude is also how you feel about yourself. You'll need a confident, positive attitude to be able to handle the severe ups and downs of a dance career.

DIFFICULTY

To become a professional dancer is so difficult I can't even begin to put it into words. I think it's safe to say that every dancer, even the very successful ones, never dreamed it would be so hard. The number of dancers competing for every job is staggering. The economy in the arts is high priced and very risky. A Broadway show carries a five to ten million dollar budget. Dance jobs are on the decline. And if that wasn't enough, you've chosen a career that has a limited length. <u>Everyone agrees,</u> don't go into the arts unless you have ability, talent, training and a passion that won't allow you to do anything else.

If you have to dance—and believe me, I understand the feeling—then do it!

Take your training, your versatility and your good attitude, and give it your best shot. There's nothing more rewarding than beating the odds and being paid for something you love to do.

I wish you the best!

INDEX

ABOUT THE AUTHOR

 Don Mirault took a dare and went to a dance class at the ripe old age of 23. The disco dance craze hit, and he found himself winning dance contests all over the country. His partner talked him into moving to Las Vegas where he immediately landed a job... going to Mexico! After six months south of the border, he returned home to perform in the "Folies Bergere". It was during the "Folies" that he became a better dancer, met his wife Sheri, and performed in many industrials, films and television specials behind stars like; Lily Tomlin, Joan Rivers, Lou Rawls, Bill Cosby, and Sammy Davis.

"A Chorus Line" rolled into Las Vegas. Don auditioned, was hired and sent to Broadway. What a break! Since then, he has performed as an actor/singer/dancer in many musicals including, Chicago, Baby, Damn Yankees, South Pacific, Can Can and many others. He's appeared on television shows such as "Golden Girls," "Star Trek – The Next Generation," "Knots Landing," "The Hogan Family" and "General Hospital." He has also worked in films like "Silver Bullet," "Kill Me Again," "Dr. Detroit" and "Drive Like Lightening." Even so, he's never forgotten his first love, dance, and the many aspects of dance he was unprepared for. Having performed in almost all the jobs discussed in this book, his advice is especially helpful.

Don believes that a career as a professional dancer is a dream worth pursuing. It is his sincere hope that with the help of this book, all of you will enjoy a terrific career in dance.

He will continue to inform the dancer in the future with revised editions of "Dancing... For A Living" including new dance jobs, more union jobs and updated information.

ORDER FORM

Rafter Publishing

11333 Moorpark Street
Suite 141
Toluca Lake, California 91602

Please send me _____ copy(s) of "Dancing... For A Living". I understand that if I'm not 100% satisfied I can return the book in good condition for a full refund. I've enclosed a check/money order payable to Rafter Publishing.

Book(s) Price .... $_____
(_____ copies X $15.95)
Shipping & Handling .... $_____
($2.00 – first book,
$0.75 – ea. addl. book)
CA Sales Tax .... $_____
($1.32 per book
CA residents only)
Air Mail (optional) .... $_____
($3.50 per book to accelerate
delivery to two weeks)
TOTAL ENCLOSED .... $_____

We will ship your order as soon as possible. Please allow four to six weeks for delivery. If you need your book sooner, please enclose an additional $3.50 per book for Air Mail.

ORDER FORM

Rafter Publishing

$15.95 Softcover